Poetry Ireland Review 129

Eagarthóir / Editor
EAVAN BOLAND

© Poetry Ireland Ltd 2019

Poetry Ireland Ltd/Éigse Éireann Teo gratefully acknowledges the assistance of The Arts Council/An Chomhairle Ealaíon and The Arts Council of Northern Ireland.

LOTTERY FUNDED

Poetry Ireland invites individuals and commercial organisations to become Patrons of Poetry Ireland. For more details, please contact:
Anne Hendrick, Development Manager,
Poetry Ireland, 11 Parnell Square East,
Dublin 1, Ireland
or telephone +353 1 6789815; e-mail development@poetryireland.ie

FOUNDING PARTNERS
Adrian Brinkerhoff Poetry Fund of the Sidney E Frank Foundation
University College Cork

POETRY PATRONS: LYRIC
Thomas Dillon Redshaw

POETRY PATRONS: SONNET
Marie Baker, Patricia Ferguson, Alan Gray, Neville Keery, John McBratney,
Joan McBreen, Marian Richardson

POETRY PATRONS: STANZA
Emer Foley, Monica McInerney

POETRY PATRONS: HAIKU
Sarah Bannan, Peter Clarke, Kevin Conroy, Richard Halperin, Susie Kennelly,
Oliver Mooney, Jean O'Brien, Andy Pollak, John Prebble, Grace Smith, Anne Tannam

ISBN: 978-1-902121-78-9   ISSN: 0332-2998

PUBLICATIONS MANAGER: **Paul Lenehan** and **Eoin Rogers**, with the assistance of
Fiona McShane and **Orla Higgins**

IRISH-LANGUAGE EDITOR: **Caitríona Ní Chléirchín**
COVER DESIGN: **Alistair Keady** (**www.hexhibit.com**)
COVER CREDIT: *Saplings* (2017) by **Ailbhe Barrett**

Contents

Editorial

This is my final issue as editor of *Poetry Ireland Review*. From start to finish, it's been an extraordinary privilege – an absorbing and memorable view of the energies and talents in the work of Irish poets and poets beyond Ireland. And now I'm delighted to turn over that view to Colette Bryce, who will bring her own poetic gifts and perspectives to the editorship.

I have some thanks to make: to Maureen Kennelly, who does so much as Director to sustain the project of Poetry Ireland and its uniquely generous relationship to the poetry community and beyond. To Paul Lenehan, who makes *Poetry Ireland Review* such a wonderfully finished journal. So much of the substance of the *Review*, from the relation of the visual to the text and the arguments to the poems, is due to him. And my special thanks to hard-working and inspiring staff like Rachel Botha and Eoin Rogers, and committed interns such as Mattie Drucker, who, with others, process the huge volume of submissions, and contribute at every stage to the publishing process.

But my chief debt, of course, is to the poets who submitted their poems. Reading them, I had the same response I've had since I was young: a response that began whenever I took a volume of poems off a shelf in a bookshop, or opened a magazine with a poem. Those pages revealed that someone had made the journey from their life to their language. Someone had followed their feelings to a form. Had gone to a blank page, maybe with the little time they had at the end of their day, not to produce an epigram but to find a truth.

Because of what I saw then, and have read since for *Poetry Ireland Review*, I've never doubted that it is working poets and the poem in its time that provide the most eloquent answer to the badly formed ideas that poetry is failing, that its audience is dwindling, that its usefulness is over.

And certainly, those comments do exist. For instance, the Australian critic who in 2005 stated the following negative view as if it was a fact: 'I'm saying three things here: that poetry has a lot of writers and not many readers, that many of the writers themselves don't read all that much, and that poetry is difficult, a lot of the time, very difficult indeed.'

Those ideas are in the air – and always familiar and unsound. The size of the audience, the difficulty of the work, these are not true measurements of an art. If used, they lure critics into memorable understatements, like the critic of Hart Crane in *The New York Times* in 1933, who commented: 'His *Collected Poems* is not an unimportant book.'

No poets – and the poets I read for *Poetry Ireland Review* illustrate this – should ever have to write or live in these shadows. The life of the poet is always a summons to try to set down some truth that was once true and will go on being true. No poet should have to worry about the public respect or the lack of it in which this art is held.

It is the poems I read in the submissions to *Poetry Ireland Review* that are a constant reminder of that. Those words on the page, those stanzas, cadences, statements, at their best, can and do lead to a single defining moment: when someone takes down a book, maybe late at night, maybe looking for some confirmation of their own life, and comes upon that poem they want to remember. That moment has held together this art from the beginning. And it always will.

– **Eavan Boland**

Patrick Slevin

NIGHT BOAT

The seats haven't changed
since last year. Bodies wash up
marooned by the news.
Someone's been at the volume.

A girl smiles – they were sat there.
Football shirts run free
down the wrong walkway, with pints,
bend their knees, wait for sea legs

then double-back. Everyone watches
the children no one's watching.
A couple stroll around the shop
for the third time, pick up the same toy,

it makes no difference
the exchange is closed.
Dawn pushes in, pale with Dublin.
Laughter drifts through the swing doors.

Eleanor Hooker

A LANDSCAPE FORFEITED TO SNOW

> *My brain hums with scraps of poetry and madness*
>   – Virginia Woolf

Centre the table beneath the mirror,
place the instruments, freshly bladed,
on the sewing bench, house suction and diathermy
in their cradles, and within reach. Tie down
the stretched, starched linen, leave no crease.
Increase the heat – blood clots readily in warm air.
Undress. Angle the light, settle yourself on the table.
Lie a moment.

A pfannenstiel incision is best, neat, along the bikini line –
you've been opened there before, for the babies.
Cut. Suction. Cauterize. Retract muscle and gut
until you reveal a landscape forfeited to snow. Wait.
Songbirds will emerge from the tear in your world,
let them fly about the room – when you return,
they will return to you, willingly. Now, venture inside.
Though you're only shadow-light, do not walk
the frozen river. For protection, carry Rowan.

Memory stains snow where it lands, follow your old track
to the lake. Careful! Don't touch – those are hands reaching
through the ice, not reeds, this is a treacherous body of water.

Aside from your birds, and the many versions of yourself
drowned in the ice, you are sole citizen, those voices
are echoes of a lifetime speaking to ghosts.

The cairn, stopped by snow, is east of you. A vast silence
echoes round it, out there where your life ends –
remove eight stones, reach in to detach your music
from the dark. Carry it back. Carry it back to the world.

It's getting late, before your birds fly back to you,
return your song to the cairn, replace the stones,
remove *all* markers – this is the fourth time
this year you've cut to that place. No more.

Gather yourself in a continuous dissolvable suture.

Ask – was it worth it?
Is the consequence hopelessness?
Entrust your melody to strangers, never your song.

Amanda Bell

*

It's
Xmas
– I'm so
triggered
I could power
each decoration
on the tree, and the
blue lights of the ambulance
the Christmas Eve Dad had a t.i.a.,
three paramedics piling in beside spiced
beef, wine spilt as glass slid from his grip, while
one hand clawed & face screwed up; at least somebody
had the *nous* to turn the telly on, distract the kids with
blinking shapes and colours while we weighed up where
to find an A & E. I hate going out at Christmas,
coming home to a cold grate; can't comprehend the sadness
that wells up so tight I feel I'll choke, spills in tears at cheesy soaps.
This dark night of the year might always be the last; we're fiercely forging
memories by the flames of table candles – yet fail
to grasp
why love
feels just
like rage

Eilis Stanley

MY SISTER'S GARDEN

We waited the waiting, my sister and I,
our circulation slowing to a centre-point of
foreboding in a hospital room of no oxygen,
diminishing hope and unspoken sentences
that hung in mid-air and dropped like hailstones
drumming out denial. Amid the broken trolleys

and curled vinyl chairs, we waited the waiting.
His nurse called us in. Her crisp uniform, a radiation
shield. I shoulder my sister, stay close, our breaths held
in the palms of a stranger and time lines up beside
him, her bearded executioner. He punches out the words,
they shatter like a saw, "a bilateral mastectomy".

And the little hands I love, break from their union, as cells
run for cover; the fire doors of her insides slamming shut.
"My nipples too?" she asks like an immigrant in her own body
locked in an innocence of registration but his mouth makes
no sound and she sits in her garden of erotic remembrance,
as the withering begins and silence settles us in her bed of loss.

Fred Johnston

1941

It was taken from the balcony, or somewhere in the gods
The row of high-kicking girls a blur of short-skirt white
As if light took its time leaving them, their leggy constellation
Rotating with infinite slowness or, arguably, light's improbable
Speed: you can tell her fourth in from the photo's right, stage-
Grinning with the rest, a tsunami of wartime rolls washing
Over the painted backdrop of a fat-winged comic airplane
Trapped in blade-sharp paper spotlights dull as smoke
The stage of The Empire Theatre full of ambush and shadows.

He played the Stage Door Johnny, so much he admitted
Together in coats blooming like parachutes in the oily wind
They'd link arms out of the Stage Entrance alley, take their
Time to a scarce taxi, canoodle in the back seat, her make-up
Powdering his double lapels, the streets under black-out rules
The scent of *Mandalay* opened his lungs like oxygen, he was
Light-headed, unsure; and if not tonight, then tomorrow
They'd come over again, cranky bombers full of fire and light
She'd be lined out in chorus high-step when the bombs fell.

Enda Wyley

SYLLABLES ON THE WIND

Mary Noonan, *Stone Girl* (Dedalus Press, 2019), €12.50.
Noel Monahan, *Chalk Dust* (Salmon Poetry, 2018), €14.
Moya Roddy, *Out of the Ordinary* (Salmon Poetry, 2018), €12.
Gabriel Fitzmaurice, *A Farewell to Poetry: Selected Poems and Translations* (Currach Books, 2019), €19.99.

The imagination as an inventive and effective tool is ever-present in *Stone Girl*, Cork poet Mary Noonan's second collection. 'The Invader' is startling for its comparing of the poet's lover to a walrus, 'bulky and clumsy and implausibly / hairy'. A dry and memorable wit reigns throughout this poem, which is also remarkably moving given that its subject is Noonan's partner, the poet Matthew Sweeney, who died in August 2018. 'Gare du Nord' has Sweeney making a heart-rending request, 'When I'm gone, you say, remember / me here.' But the thought of his imminent death is too overpowering for the poet, whose thoughts reach an affecting conclusion – one reflected in the collection's title:

> Do you really think I could look again
> at these end-of-the-line pillars and porticoes,
> these blind granite women, remembering you,
> and not myself be turned to stone?

Other poems also bear witness to stone statues of women. There's the statue of the Virgin Mary in 'Hail, Holy Queen', carried by 'gentlemen of the / *hermandades*', through the streets of Seville at Easter to the bullring. There's the 'stone women of Paris', in 'Caryatids', the most notable of these is Rodin's, like a 'banished angel reduced to human scale: / a girl. Crouching on the artist's plinth'. And there's the tragedy of Camille Claudel in 'Clotho', who 'grew into the scandal' she had sculpted – 'an old woman, deciding nothing'.

Noonan is a lecturer in French Literature in University College Cork, and Paris is understandably a vibrant character within the folds of this book. In 'Rue St Paul', she brilliantly captures how embarrassed she felt about her parents' visit to her in Paris, years before. She remembers 'their unfashionable clothes and poor hair-cuts', and is critical of her behaviour towards them: 'I hope I was kind to them, but I doubt it.'

A dominant force in the book is her parents' life together. In 'Kensington High Street', the poet exits the Underground in rush hour and conjures up the memory of her mother and father in the 1950s, 'too poor to marry in Fermoy', escaping to London. Her mother's presence is haunting: 'You're here, / twenty-five, hurrying to the tube that will whisk you / / to the Opera, to your narrow seat in the gods.'

Stone Girl is also fuelled by many fine elegies for Noonan's father. 'Body' evocatively begins, 'We never touched, all the years / of our long story, kept our distance.' It is a distance narrowed by her shaving and washing of her father, her putting him to bed – all captured with unwavering honesty. 'I never thought I'd see / my father's penis. And after the long haul / of hours spent cajoling you to lie down / under the covers, you grab my hand, / lock it in yours, won't let it go.' The tenacity of these final lines is indicative of the admirable resolve evident throughout *Stone Girl*. This is a collection which determinedly pays imaginative and heartfelt homage to life's joys and losses, in poems that possess their own unique voice and ultimately ring true.

'Chalk Dust', the powerful title poem of Noel Monahan's eighth collection, vividly depicts the misery of life in a Catholic boarding school in Cavan in the sixties. But thankfully, the poem also offers moments of joy, all memorably described. Spicer's delivery van came once a week: 'Deep in the back shelves, we invariably found the creamy buns and stuffed our pockets full.' Mrs Owens, the 'oven goddess', would appear on her bicycle, 'one of the few women seen about the college and we took time out to see her come and go'. The poet also remembers in great detail his triumphant schoolmates when they beat *'the Armagh boys'*, at football:

> Fr Fither gave us free time in Armagh. Some of us played the machines. We
> bought shilling shares in another Playboy. Some of us smoked Gallaghers'
> Blues. Others ran down alleyways after convent girls.

'Chalk Dust' is episodic, following the school's calendar. With the arrival of spring, 'the allure of the trees was great'. School days are temporarily forgotten, and we sense in the lyrical section, 'To The Woods And The River', an awakening of a young poet whose descriptive powers are on a par with those of Patrick Kavanagh:

> Those were dreamy moments of joy, looking across at the hump of a hill,
> with two legs of ditches dipping into the gush of water, *Toor-a loor-a loora* ...

Kavanagh's influence on Noel Monahan's development as a poet is further apparent in the opening section, 'The Corleck Head'. In the fine and heart-breaking poem, 'Response to a Billhead, 1944', lyrical place-names – Coolagherty, Muckerstaff, Killeen – are listed as a backdrop to the hardships of his parents' rural life. But his mother is determined to 'make the marriage at Kenagh work / To take life beyond the fields and men, / To build an altar of love on the landing'.

The life she creates, described in another poem, 'Doing the Rounds', is dominated by the rituals and traditions of religion – 'Reciting prayers, verses, drinking / From wells, kissing stones, hugging trees'. But Monahan is quick to differentiate between these rituals and 'the jealous and vengeful church', in his passionate 'Hymn for the Tuam Babies', which demands that we 'raise the baby bones to the light'.

The twenty-five sonnets in the section 'Stone-Breaker' are finely wrought and thematically diverse. Religion is present again, but it serves only as a means to praise the poet's world. Here, the stand-out poems are inspired by grandchildren and by responses to paintings by Picasso, Pádraig Lynch, and Bartolome Esteban Murillo.

Noel Monahan's talent as an Irish-language poet and translator flowers in 'Dánta i nGaeilge agus Aistriúcháin' / 'Poems in Irish and Translations'. His poetry is highly visual and at its best honours the pared back beauty of a simple image:

> Séideann an oíche
> Siollaí gaoithe ag seinm
> Gan fhios dom.

> The night is playing
> Syllables on the wind
> Without my knowing.
>   – 'TAOBH AMUIGH TAOBH ISTIGH' / 'ON THE OUTSIDE AND INSIDE'

Chalk Dust is the work of a consummate and established poet, as proven in this varied, skilled, and thoroughly enjoyable collection.

The intimacies of mother and daughter relationships in their many forms are ever present in Moya Roddy's engaging *Out of the Ordinary*. In the opening poem, the daughter-narrator matter-of-factly tells how she would come home from school most afternoons to find her mother 'on the living-room couch / buried beneath a mound of coats'. But at five o'clock there would come a shift; the mum suddenly getting up, to 'sally forth / to get something in for tea /… as if you'd just risen from the dead'. Honesty, vulnerability, and surprise are key elements in this poem, 'Miracle', and prove to be three of the most vital traits of Roddy's work throughout this collection.

Roddy is also determined to untangle her mother's personal history and to unearth hidden truths. A visit to a killeen in Killary proves devastating in the poem 'Limbo', the poet's mother articulating for the first time her grief for the loss of three of her children: '*Oh my babies, my babies,* / she cries, tears running down her face.' But Roddy is also a mother herself, her role inspiring several emotionally charged poems.

Her child springs 'like a hare from the trap' in 'Kindling', heading off on the school bus in 'a stiff new uniform'. She is 'branching out', and it is hard not to feel for the poet negotiating this life-changing moment, while also struggling to gift her daughter the freedom that is an important part of growing up. When her daughter does eventually leave home, the poem 'She's Leaving Home', is lonely and heart-breaking all at once; 'Turn down that music, I shout, my voice / echoing through the silent house.'

Other striking poems in this collection are those highly visual ones that once read, are hard to forget. A dead hare found on the road rises from its 'makeshift grave' and springs into the poet's dreams ('A Dead Hare'). Clothes on a line, on a frosty night, are 'like dried / fruit or the cast-off skins of aliens' ('Bringing in the Washing'). A grieving sister reaches for the binoculars of her dead brother; 'When at last I raised them to my eyes / all I could see was a blur' ('His World'). A young girl is teased by the children on her street for her family's rural background – 'Wasn't I asking for it – / with my red hair, a heart / open as a country road' ('The Girls on my Street').

But it is to her mother again that this collection finally returns in the penultimate poem 'Curtain Call':

> The day the consultant made his final prognosis,
>   she opened her arms to him –
>   sang.

Out of the Ordinary is true to its title, finding in the everyday much to be inspired by – tender moments laid bare with honesty and heart.

Gabriel Fitzmaurice, in his introduction to *A Farewell to Poetry: Selected Poems and Translations*, says: 'This, I feel, is my final book. The job is done. In the words of Saint Paul; "I have fought a good fight, I have finished my course, I have kept the faith."' This selection showcases decades of Fitzmaurice's poetry, from his debut collection *Rainsong*, in 1984, through to *Smitten Soul* (2018), including his uncollected poems, and is the work of one who has undoubtedly 'kept the faith' – exemplified by a wide variety of poetry in English for both adults and children, poems in Irish, and translations of Irish-language poets such as Dáibhí Ó Bruadair, Michael Hartnett, and Caitlín Maude.

Fintan O'Toole, in his foreword to this book, astutely describes Fitzmaurice as 'one of the last of the tribal bards, a poet in and of his own kind'. Born in Moyvane, Co Kerry, the poet is steadfast in his celebration of the small village he hails from – its people, stories, traditions, and rituals. As such, *A Farewell to Poetry* makes for a fine gathering of poems. Especially striking, to this reviewer, are the intensely felt elegies to Fitzmaurice's parents. The memory of his father shouldering coffins of family members, in 'Requiescat,' elicits from the poet this tender response:

> And as we lowered you, father,
> A generation knew
> That the time had come for passing on.
> Now I inherit you.

Family is integral to Fitzmaurice's work. In 'Sonnet to Brenda,' he describes poetry as 'the only thing that's constant in my life', and compares it to the enduring nature of his marriage: 'The iambic heart that pulses in these lines / Measures out my love. And it still rhymes.'

The Irish language is integral to his work as a poet. 'Gaeltacht' ends effusively, 'But this was love, was Irish, and was bliss.' There are skilful translations by Fitzmaurice of iconic Irish poems – 'Cill Chais', 'The Yellow Bittern', 'The Spailpín Fánach', 'Cill Aodáin', to name a few – many of these poems concerned with the plight of the poet, best articulated in Raftery's 'I am Raftery':

> Look at me now,
> My back to a wall,
> Playing music
> For empty pockets.

Throughout *A Farewell to Poetry* there is a profound awareness of the transience of life, and of the poet's historical place in the generations of Moyvane's Fitzmaurices.

> I'm the last Fitzmaurice
> Still here where we began,
> The name will die out with me
> When I'm buried in Moyvane.

In his introduction, the poet describes how the last line of a sonnet came unexpectedly to him in the noisy play area of Crag Cave, Castleisland, Co Kerry, where he was surrounded by his wife and grandchildren: 'And immediately I sensed that this would probably be the last poem I would have to write.'

'Out of the Abyss' may in fact be his final poem, but there is great comfort to be found in Gabriel Fitzmaurice's *A Farewell to Poetry*, where a fine selection of his work remains and will endure.

Francis O'Hare

A BREATH OF SEA

in memoriam Padraic Fiacc, 1924–2019

In the rain-dark
Belfast night
of the soul,
newborn-stark,
your poems took flight
through an evil

odour of blood
that soured the air
like a stain,
a mist-mould
of black despair,
wound-raw pain,

rising up
from burnt out
backstreet scenes,
the last gasp
of a victim shot
behind some bins,

metallic screams
of 'pigs' round corners
into mazes
of tear-gas, fumes,
brutal soldiers
raiding houses,

kids dragged out
of duckdown beds
and into cells
where warders shut
steel doors on anguished
shrieks and howls,

stutter-sobs
of *miserere*
as hoods were lowered,
raging mobs,
red-eyed rioter,
the known code-word

in a phone-call
to the BBC
before a bomb,
the bland, civil
hypocrisy
of officialdom

as the grey smoke
of morning cleared
over dead
bodies, baked,
blasted, charred
as skin roasted

in hell-fire,
up towards
the heavenlight
like birds, desire,
leaves, rosebuds
of prayer, dew-bright –

Padraic Fiacc,
you dared to utter
transcendental
psalms like Blake
cried in the gutter
of the real

and forged us wings
to soar above
the unreal city,
your broken songs
of heartache, love,
a breath of sea.

Jack Coughlan

DIASPORA

It wasn't like Abraham leaving his own people and his father's house,
taking his goats and his Sara and his phimosis with him;
not like Moses escaping from Egypt
or the wild geese flying to France
to make brandy and fight foreign wars.
In fact, it was like nothing, there was no event.

We were working, earning money and
we just forgot the time. At first, we
weren't aware that the parsnips, the
brown bread and the rhubarb tart were missing.
Noticing, we also began missing
the trees where our memories nested,
the streets and the fields they were prowling,
fences, hedges and gates they were tied to.

The people were mostly friendly. They talked
about Joyce and The Dubliners and
they praised the ring of Kerry,
but they had never heard of hurling.
They wanted to hear our songs
in their strange land.
They were out of tact with us, tactless
at times where we were awkward.

We learned their language. The words
were easy but there was no room
between the lines and our meanings
didn't fit.
We noticed that we weren't normal.
We weren't as intelligent as we used to be.
We tried to be more of what we had been
than we had ever been. We were strained.

We were welcomed home after nearly
a long time, but of course nobody had
waited for us. Their lives happened
without us. Our accents had changed.
Things were different.

We noticed that we weren't normal.
We were Rip van Winkles,
but not really back; just visiting.

You can't commute between
Used to be and is now,
you get lost in transit or arrive
as a familiar stranger. You feel
strange too, of a different kind.
The fields of Athenry can't cure that,
the gatherings don't know it; we'll
surely doubly die here, unwept.

Marie Herbert

OLD PAIN AS WELL AS NEW

Your features contort at the news
of your grandchild
growing inside me;
a competition you can't win.

You shudder at my excitement
at the kicks of life
and your skin crawls while my skin stretches
and you turn away while I catch elbows, feet and fists.

I thought it could be different
once their fingers had held yours
but now this third time
I can't help but fill the pain of your silence
with my own.

Catherine Gander

SINGING IN DARK TIMES

Erika Meitner, *Holy Moly Carry Me* (BOA Editions, 2018), $17.
Tracy K Smith, *Eternity: Selected Poems* (Penguin Books, 2019), £10.99.

Erika Meitner's fifth poetry collection, *Holy Moly Carry Me*, contains multitudes. Interweaving the lyric and the epic, the self and the social, the book bears witness to the manifold perils, demands, and anxieties of living in twenty-first century America – as a child of an immigrant and a refugee amid rising conservative attitudes toward the stateless; as a Jew in an increasingly anti-Semitic political climate; as the mother of one white son and one Black son in a country with an ongoing history of racist violence; as a parent whose neighbours keep firearms; as a professor in a university that in 2007 saw the deadliest school shooting in US history. Expansive and transhistorical, yet rooted in the current moment, Meitner's is a poetry of accretion. Line by line, the poems in this urgent book gather objects, lives, bodies, and moments to each other to reveal the necessity of our interconnections, and the dangers of overlooking them.

The American lineage of such an aesthetics of attention can be traced through Frank O'Hara to Walt Whitman – both of whom get a nod in Meitner's book – but in these poems, attention assumes a quality more akin to what Simone Weil recognised as the purest form of generosity. 'Attention, taken to its highest degree, is the same thing as prayer', Weil wrote in *Gravity and Grace*. 'It presupposes faith and love.' Every poem in this open-hearted, clear-eyed collection is thus a prayer; a call and a response to the luminous particulars of everyday life. 'Bless the black G-string, / abandoned on the sidewalk', begins 'Post-Game-Day-Blessing', a poem that picks through the detritus of the morning after in a touchingly loving liturgy of the hopeful and the discarded. Meitner's speaker is on route to the library with a group of first graders, but she's also stepping through the capitalist clutter of contemporary America, a participant-observer and chaperone along the interlacing roads that make up the country.

In the exquisite opening poem 'HolyMolyLand', Meitner at once unravels and braids together the sacred and profane meanings of its title. The poem unfolds the consequences of faith and devotion like a Jacob's ladder, each step a foothold amid the slippage that occurs between inter-pretations of the pure and sacrosanct. From the start, Meitner signposts that the journey we are about to embark upon is both epic and personal:

> In *The Odyssey* there's mention of a plant called moly, which is sacred and
> harvested only by the gods.

> The gods are vengeful but they are also good to us, though we have given up
> sacrifices and burnt offerings.
>
> With regard to burnt offerings, the following is a concise statement of
> the Levitical law: these were wholly animal, and the victims were wholly
> consumed.

The 'burnt offerings' haunt the concentration camps of Meitner's family history, which surfaces often in the book to test another Levitical law: that one must love one's neighbour as oneself. Each prose stanza provides another link in the associative chain of what we hold most dear – freedom, memories, expression, faith, family, home – pushing their definitions to ultimately probe 'the space between the hole and the holy, the torn passports, desperation and possibility'.

Elsewhere, threshold spaces hold the fear and grief of bodily absence. The book is shot through with the pain of Meitner's infertility, the room within her own body that refuses, this time, to germinate life. Children are at the heart of this collection, and Meitner explores the spaces, both safe and dangerous, that we ask them to inhabit. Halfway through the collection is a second 'HolyMolyLand' – 'a place we all pass through (of violence, of revelation)'. Perhaps the most sombre of the collection, the poem points to the ways in which 'we inscribe the darkest days of history on our own bodies'. In limber lines that flex with multiple meanings, this central poem links the protection strategies of Holocaust survivors, who 'played their faded numbers in the / lottery or used them as passwords' to the active shooter drills at Meitner's son's school ('*I would take my friends & hide, he says. I would be very quiet*'). Our hiding places reveal missing struts in the architecture of our humanity, gaps textually echoed in the poem's perforated prayer: 'Holy is the _____ of _____.' What to do, Meitner asks across this astonishing collection, when the blanks become the background noise to living – the 'sounds of the shooting range up the road'? In times like these, how precarious the border between the blank and the bullet, the startling sound and the silence that follows.

Yet despite the gravity of her subject-matter, Meitner guides her reader with a warmth and wit that extend a feeling of hope in human action. *Holy Moly Carry Me*'s poetics of accretion may reflect late stage capitalism's logic of accumulation, but it also reflects the myriad ways our lives accrue meaning and strength. There is no such thing as 'too strong', Meitner reminds us in the poem of the same name, so that one might 'look into the gaping maw / of the beast that eats your sons— / the lion, the bullets, the streets, racist / cops, heroin, despair, whatever is most / predatory and say, *Enough—we will triumph, / motherfuckers*.'

The triumph will come via the sense of community that Meitner's deeply generous poems generate. While the chain-link image of 'Holy-

MolyLand' reflects the 'holes in all of these stories – open-mouthed gaps in the fence, a singing presence', the book's final poem reshapes the barrier as 'a human chain', 'a neon OPEN sign / singing into the night' – an image of collective resistance and solidarity that recalls Bertolt Brecht's famous poem 'Motto' ('In the dark times / Will there also be singing? / Yes, there will also be singing. / About the dark times'). *Holy Moly Carry Me* is singing in the dark times, and a necessary gift from a poet in full command of her voice.

The space-time sweep of Tracy K Smith's *Eternity: Selected Poems*, transports the reader through a constellation of poems that both punctuate the dark areas of American history and hold the beauty of human existence to the light. If eternity is a timeless realm, shaped by emotional need, and populated by gods, then poetry is its portal. Smith's writing has remained, from her debut collection, *The Body's Question* (2003), to her most recent *Wade in the Water* (2018), an exploration of the avenues toward that portal, and the questions that turn its key.

In *The Body's Question*, Smith explores the contours of our corporeal existence, tracing the impulses that join bodies, for better or worse, across historical and spatial dimensions. 'Bright' imagines, with dreamy lucidity, the arrival of Portuguese colonisers on 'restless waves' to Cape Bianco; their incredulity at the sight of 'Lean bodies ... Like the deep / Center of the darkest fruit':

> The first fig. Primordial.
> Not sin – not yet –
> But satisfaction. Black
> As the space between stars ...

Smith continues, 'bodies, / Like mine / Or any other –', before retracing these short steps: 'No: like mine / But intact'. The poem establishes a theme that threads throughout *Eternity*: that darkness can be dazzling. Here, it is genesis, an energy collapsing distances between cosmological birth, biblical beginnings, and a terrestrial aboriginality unscarred by notions of sin, and by the brutality so often enacted by white bodies upon black.

Returning to these early poems, we see taking shape what we now associate with Smith: a deft and sensuous weave of the grand themes of our existence with the objects of the everyday, performed with both a warm brilliance and a cool ease that belies the complexity of her craft. 'Bright' begins with a contemplation of a bowl of marinated catfish, and concludes wondering 'if you and I // Have not, perhaps, / Beheld one another ... Elsewhere, and / before.' 'Shadow Poem' digs deeper into creation and death, drawn by the tidal pull of the book's recurrent primal images, and entwining the lyric 'I' and the imagined 'you' in unconstrained relation: 'We were souls together once / Wave after wave of ether / Alive outside of time'.

Writing in the wake of grief for her late mother, Smith suggests in 'Joy' that the body is mobilised by a question: 'What do you believe in?' Belief – religious, spiritual, interpersonal – pervades the pages of this book, bound tightly to its eternal twin, need. Indeed, *Duende* (2007) and the Pulitzer-winning *Life on Mars* (2011) seem to hum with a human need to connect – to others, to oneself, to something larger than either, or both, of these. Amid such vast yearnings, Smith's poems provide means rather than meaning. They recall Muriel Rukeyser's oft-quoted line that the universe is made of stories, not atoms. And they ask us to listen.

Duende's long poem 'History' is 'a story in the poem's own voice'; a free verse 'epic' tuned to a frequency both astrophysical and earthly. Reading it is like watching the history of the world on a time-lapse. Glimpses of beauty and pain flash past; the iris of the poem widens and contracts between the immense and the minute. 'Once there was a great cloud / Of primeval matter. Atoms and atoms', Smith writes. 'By believing, we made it the world. ... Made ourselves human out of need.' Smith recognises the majesty and the misery in such a design; that need can be an eternal loop of hunger without satisfaction – a snake swallowing its own tail.

Several poems across the selection explore the darker definition of need as privation. Written in the voice of the Ho-Chunk Indian, John Dall, who in 1963 'was taken from his mother's home as part of a federal project to reduce poverty in Native American communities', *Duende*'s 'Theft' motions toward the grim irony – read: lie – in that official justification, but avoids holding to account those whose 'project' is driven by the need to dehumanise. While such poems stitch true stories into the fabric of the book's universe, the expansive aesthetic and overriding empathy that compels much of its first half at times have the effect of rendering these stories fairly weightless in the greater scheme of things. Amid the epic arc of 'History', Smith appears to caution against 'political' poetry: 'Of course there are victims in this poem', she writes, before inserting the words *'you are here'* into a text block built of the word, 'victim'.

Life on Mars extends the galactic wonder of Smith's first two collections, freighting it with a gravity that connects the reader more concretely to immediate social realities. The gorgeous 'My God, It's Full of Stars' sweeps the reader up in its arching vision of the numerous ways we picture the great beyond – via movies, daydreams, Smith's late father's work on the Hubble Telescope – and reminds us that despite these images essentially being self-portraits, 'Perhaps the great error is believing we're alone'. Elsewhere, Smith's tone dips to describe dystopias more vivid than those on the silver screen. Dark matter is drained of its radiance in 'Life on Mars'; it's now 'the space between people', the tenor of terror in practices of protection and surveillance. The poem remembers the news story of a man who serially raped his daughter while keeping her and their children in a cage. He moved through the world 'like a god'; 'They begged him for air, and all he saw were bodies on their knees.' Another sobering section is comprised solely of lines taken from media sources discussing the abuse of detainees by US military personnel at Abu Ghraib prison: 'I'm only talking about people / Having a good time, blowing off steam.'

'They May Love All That He Has Chosen and Hate All That He Has Rejected' provides a poignant twist to the sci-fi trope of messages from the unknown: a sequence of postcards from the victims of hate crimes to their murderers, sent from US landmarks. It's here that Smith's concern with problems particularly American crystallises. As in 'The Universe is a House Party', whose couplets laced with irony – *Mi casa es su casa. Never more sincere'* – convey the double standards of a nation that prides itself on hospitality, Smith's lines lead to a deepening political engagement. In *Wade in the Water*, the collection published during her time as US Poet Laureate, Smith turns her lens fully in the direction of the States.

As one might expect from Smith, the last poems in *Eternity* point to beginnings – indeed, the selection starts with 'Garden of Eden'. Yet in these poems, Smith, now at the height of her powers, excavates spaces of American history to reveal the ongoing nature of the past's aggressions and injustices, especially against immigrants and people of colour. One of the most quietly devastating poems is 'Declaration', an erasure poem from the text of the Declaration of Independence:

> He has plundered our –

> ravaged our –

> destroyed the lives of our –

> [...]

> We have reminded them of the circumstances of our emigration and settlement here.

> – taken Captive

> on the high Seas

> to bear –

Rehearsing the nation's erasure of Black lives and liberties, and weighted by what it doesn't say, the poem speaks in the voices of the beaten down and dispossessed with a rhythm as insistent as waves on the shoreline of the New World.

The collection's central poem sequence also sees Smith take on the role of curator (from the Latin *cura*, to take care) to address issues of race, historicity, and belonging. 'I Will Tell You the Truth About This, I Will Tell You All About It' is a series of found poems: Civil War era letters from enlisted slaves and their families, requesting the return of relatives, or payments long since owed. The voices of these men and women increase in urgency and number, until their pleas to be heard crowd the pages, clear, strong, and strikingly present. Smith's touch here is exceedingly light, and yet almost palpably loving.

Indeed, love, reaffirmed in the African American ring-shout that gives the collection its name, pierces through these poems, eclipsing need, to become the book's binding energy: 'I love you, she said. She didn't / Know me, but I believed her'. For Smith, love is both the force behind and the answer to the body's initial question of belief, 'a language / Few practice but all, or near all, speak' ('Unrest in Baton Rouge'). Like the water that serves as the book's central metaphor, we can choose to poison it or we can wade in it, baptise one another with it. Across this splendid selection, Smith practises love's language with the warmth and luminosity of the water that ends her remarkable poem 'Watershed', seeking, in the way that perhaps only poetry enables, 'the most connection with the eternal'.

Nicola Healey

SWEET PEA

> *And yet it was a seed which, had it found,*
> *By river's brink or rocky mountain cleft,*
> *A kindly shelter and a genial ground,*
> *Might not have perish'd ...*
> — Hartley Coleridge

At the back of her wardrobe
my mum found decade-old seeds
saved from a sweet pea.
Shrivelled-up, hard grey pellets.

We hydrated them and planted them
more on a whim than belief,
though, in a desolate land,
I did align all hope with theirs.

I watched their ground daily until
a millimetre of green appeared;
then more and more – each new shoot,
tendril and sunlit petal

audacious with elegant proof
of the intricate regions of the invisible
and of silence,
and a seed's locked faith

in being unlocked.
One Tyrian purple flower
held the room in fragile majesty;
its scent transcended it –

first slight, then unending.

Aoife Reilly

GENESIS

after Kaylin Haught

After the fifth hole on the second day
the god of the drill spoke.
She said it was absolutely fine
about the multiple injuries to the kitchen wall.
Make as many holes as you need.
And when I drove in that pz2 screw
which seemed to hit major resistance,
then proceeded to cover all extra holes
with my origami fox, winking just over the biggest one,
god said that was ok too, be creative, why not?
When I cursed myself for not listening
to anything mechanically related in school
and called the wall stupid,
which was followed by a bout of bitterness
in the face of no rescue, she declared I should adopt
an attitude of gratitude. Good that I didn't get electrocuted
in the face of hardcore feminism with drill bits.
(She said it was ok to call that feminism too if I wanted).

When I worried about the years of possible disasters to come,
she just said, look loveen, in the beginning
light was day, dark was night, the vault between
a canvas destined for cracks.
Go live your life.

Supriya Kaur Dhaliwal

HOUSING CRISIS ON RAGLAN ROAD

During my early teenage years,
when I was old enough to learn big words –
I thought solitude was soltitude. The extra *t* a sword
to cut through a lapsed state of being on one's own. It appears,
maybe, like a briny situation in the mouth that prefers
the taste of days spent alone. Was it solitude's better byword
for a happier state of mind? Was it a watchword
for failed solitude, the worst of all our fears?

In Dublin, on a day as grey as if smeared with pewter,
I think of Kavanagh while walking through Raglan Road
and his poem of the same name. I think of no kin, no suitor.
I think of the debt these houses have owed
to the people who every day in this city seek recruiters
for new jobs with no solitude or soltitude or abode.

Enda Wyley

SOLAR ECLIPSE

  – for Janet Mullarney

Take a chance. Knock. You might be
let in through that wooden door.

Step carefully but do not be afraid.
He only wants to startle you –

peacock on the kitchen floor,
who flew from Ravenna

and landed here, to strut
below the pomegranate tree.

Indigo blue and emerald green,
this bird of linoleum marquetry –

his eye a fallen fruit, ruby red,
curious within his tiny head.

Take a chance. Go there so you may
know the quiet square, the white door

and how, after the moon has passed
between sun and earth,

sudden light will strike
the lamellae of this bird –

a thousand coloured spots
shimmering on the kitchen floor.

Jocelyn Casey-Whiteman

SEA DREAM

Besides the sigh of waves, the shore is quiet.
  Flat, jade trees of seaweed trace a forest in the sand.
Shells are vacant hotels, scrubbed to a clear, pink shine.

  My lace hem heavy, soaked with salt and fish thoughts.
Shellfish snapped dark clouds on the ocean floor.
  I slip oysters further into the sand so no one will shuck

their pearls. *What is love*, I ask the puffin who joins me
  by the water's edge. I kneel, she perches on my lap,
my skin softens. Each time the sea rinses over us, we sink

  a little. Her eyes are buttons sewn deep into her mind.
Sun turns the clouds tangerine. The water rushes, sloshes,
  stings, but the puffin looks stoic. Her head smells of kelp.

A wave tosses us, the vista switches –
  sea up-sky-down-sky-side-sand-down – help!
says my head. When the wave finally lets go,

  I feel the ground like an elevator arriving.
The world kaleidoscopes. I crawl through
  the smell of bayberry and chimney smoke,

try to catch my breath. *Smack, smack*
  the puffin waddles toward me.
My dress is torn from finding the god in everything.

Beverley Bie Brahic

EDUARDO

Eduardo cannot stay on task.
While his teacher spits-and-polishes
A few nuggets of English vocab
For the Small Group, Eduardo vaults
The window and ambles off
Towards the river and villages
Whose lanes and orchard walls
The Impressionists painted
Again and again, determined
To record each change in the light.

In the bag with the supplies
He packs to school each day –
Matches, tinder – Eduardo keeps a story
About a prospector in the Yukon
Who freezes to death on the trail
With night falling, his matches gone,
And an unreadable dog.

Niamh Nic Ghabhann

BY HEART

Lavinia Greenlaw, *The Built Moment* (Faber and Faber, 2019), £14.99 hb.
Jo Slade, *Cycles and Lost Monkeys* (Salmon Poetry, 2019), €12.
Nessa O'Mahony, *The Hollow Woman On The Island* (Salmon Poetry, 2019), €12.

Words take on a specific urgency during times of illness and bereavement – they can become the hook on which all hope is caught, endlessly turned over and examined for days on end. They can land in the space between two people like a brick careening through a window – unwanted, shocking, utterly disturbing. They can be votive, a rolling wave of sound – 'our life, our sweetness, and our hope; to thee do we cry, poor banished children of Eve, to thee do we send up our sighs'. It's at such times that the social value of words learned by heart becomes very evident, what Jeanette Winterson has called 'mental furniture' that is simply there to rely on at a time of chaos. The work, however, of writing about sickness, the failing body, death, and grief, eschews that existing mental furniture to chart the experience again, to record it and to render it in new ways.

Lavinia Greenlaw's *The Built Moment* includes a sequence that charts her father's dementia, titled 'The sea is an edge and an ending'. The poems move between a relational register (the father observed from the perspective of the poet-daughter, their relationship in focus), and a more observational register, observing the father, closely describing his condition and experience. Occasionally, as in 'His diagnosis', Greenlaw positions the poem as reflective of her father's interior experience, juxtaposing time periods, images, and ideas to create a frightening bricolage, at the end of which the barely-registered 'important news' is heard in the darkness. This intimacy of perspective allows Greenlaw to communicate the small terrors of her father's increasing frailty and loss of control with great power, as in 'He scares me', and 'My father's weakness'. In the latter poem, the image of the father – once 'talking or drawing the talk towards himself', now simply sitting among the conversation, 'his eyes following the noise / as if we were animals grappling for meat', and 'working hard to go unnoticed / to be allowed to remain' – is drawn from that intimacy between the father and daughter, a deep familial knowledge that is then made available to the reader in all its painful clarity.

Throughout, Greenlaw uses images of heavy machinery, labour, and war to convey a sense of the danger and fear involved in the experience of dementia and loss. In 'My father remembers', for example, memory is not light or incorporeal, but is a cargo afloat, a dockyard under water, in which the 'crane's hook swings to and fro / grabbing whatever is bumped within reach'. In 'My father cannot stop', the mind is an engine falling apart, and in 'My father rises whenever', his mind is an image of 'bombed streets and brute structures', with 'uncoupled engines / shunting themselves up and down brief tracks'. These physical, heavy images resurface in the second half of the collection, in the 'shocked engine' of 'The break', and in 'A time when work was visible', and 'Desynchronosis'.

Finally, this sequence is patterned with ideas of darkness and light, a kind of imagistic chiaroscuro. In the initial poems, it is the father who dwells in darkness, walking out into a storm of grief. '*There*, he says, as we turn each black corner' ('There, he says'), or stumbling in his comprehension, when he 'tries to leave the dark room but this time steps out into more darkness' ('His diagnosis'). Towards the end of the sequence, however, it is her father that moves into an unrelenting light, one that is both dangerous and relieving for him, and she is the one who is in the shadows. In 'My father rises whenever', she asks 'Is it never dark for him now?', as he wanders from his house into the night. This lightening and lightness involves the shedding of personal items ('And so he keeps arriving / in loose parcels he wraps as a gift' in 'His gifts'), the abandonment of secrecy ('My father on paper') and of shame or self-awareness ('Four days, three nights'), and leaving his home ('His home comes apart at the touch'). At the end of the sequence, Greenlaw creates an image of her father's loss of memory as a flattening, his 'unshadowed self' (in 'My father has no shadow') part of the ritual of his body moving towards death. In 'His freedom', this chiaroscuro is brought to the fore, with the 'crowded darkness' in contrast with her father who 'stands free, locked into brightness. / His world is wonderful', recalling the figures in a Cimabue painting that exist beyond the viewer, unavailable for intercession, and in a state of transcendence.

This ekphrastic suggestion points to the painterly quality of several of the poems throughout the book ('Yellow, lichen', in particular). 'A panorama for and of my father', for instance, attends to qualities of space, depth, and light, establishing verticals, horizontals, and the stilled fall of light across the scene. This poem is mirrored in 'The bluebell horizontal', a short, three-line poem that quickly sketches a tight picture, depth and light deftly established:

> Deep woods.
> Bright shallows overwhelming
> a crowd of vertical tensions.

The spatial, near-sculptural qualities of many of the poems in this collection is suggested in its title, but the title poem takes this further. Here, the artefact of the poem (something 'built') stands in as an article of faith. This complex poem presents the reader with the challenge of wishing for form, for faith, but finding it elusive and magical, 'finding at its centre a small but infinite ravine' ('The built moment'). The final pages of Greenlaw's collection reflects the space between the poem as an edifice, as the construction of something with density, form, and a relation to the world as lived (an article of faith – 'Fleur de sel'), and the work, the heavy lifting, involved in that construction process, suggested in the halting, anxious lexicon of the final poem, 'A difficulty with words'.

Jo Slade's collection, *Cycles and Lost Monkeys* opens with a journey in an indeterminate space. The initial carefree atmosphere – cycling in the woods towards home, a tune in the air – is undermined almost immediately with notes of darkness – 'Abandonment-baby', a 'genocide of wheels / and chains', and the image of memory as a 'derelict cinema / with red velvet seats and a hole in the wall / where an eye festers' ('Cycles and Lost Monkeys'). This sense of the uncanny echoes throughout this allusive and evocative collection, which ranges across different physical, temporal, and emotional territories. Although there are some specific places mentioned – Raqqa, Birkenau, Buenos Aires, and Berlin – there are no clear markers as to where the poet is situated, or precisely how she relates to the specific ideas and images that are invoked throughout. Indeed, several of the poems chart a severe sense of dislocation, of the poet being 'locked into / my skull dark with imaginings' ('I see them in the distance'), while the souls of the dead seem more real than she does. This kind of travel between time zones and places repeats as a motif throughout the collection, with Slade using words deftly to conjure a sense of movement. In 'After such a fall', Slade writes that 'She'll slip like a lip through a vacant lot / if you don't stop her', the falling vowel sounds mimicking the downward spiral of the subject of the poem. In 'Underground', the speaker within the poem exists within the London underground, waiting for a 'carriage of children', until 'A torch blazed a hole in the earth / I climbed up and like a seed / drifted into the world', while 'Palimpsest' brings us to images of bodies washed up on the shores of the Mediterranean. Images of lost, endangered, or dangerous children recur throughout the collection, acting as a source of anxiety rather than hope.

The over-arching atmosphere of *Cycles and Lost Monkeys* is one of grief and loss. In poems such as 'I'm writing a way through winter', and 'Someone', emotional states are rendered legible with great clarity. In 'Someone', the pervasive sense of urgent pain is reflected through the tree that is 'sore to the sound of timber', as someone nearby saws wood for a barricade. In 'I turn my back on the world', the vulnerability of the speaker is communicated via the sudden and violent image of the 'tidal-bat of ignominy' which cracks off her back, submerging her in the news of war from around the world, the 'abysmal days common tortures'. While 'Someone' succeeds through its precise, nuanced clarity, the collection as a whole risks being submerged by its collecting of too many griefs from the news of the day (Homs, Raqqa, the refugee crisis in the Mediterranean), and the flash points of the past – mothers looking for their disappeared sons in the Plaza de Mayo, and the horrors of the concentration camps in 'Birkenau' and 'Sisters'. The sustained register of high emotional urgency and melancholia across the collection can be somewhat disorienting, flattening specificity in the onslaught of description. By contrast, the short prose poems, including 'Light' and 'Zero', allow Slade to demonstrate her skill in crafting succinct and resonant worlds through precise description and the careful opening out of larger questions drawn from the moment at hand.

Like Greenlaw's *The Built Moment*, Nessa O'Mahony's *The Hollow Woman on the Island* is a collection that intimately charts the experience of illness, loss and faith. It's a collection that is located in the present moment, speaking to the everyday as well as the extraordinary. *The Hollow Woman on the Island* opens in an observational register, remembering historic events on the 'sleety 60s streets' as viewed through 'Snow-flickered images on our TV screens', but by the end of 'Bogeyman' the reader is brought to the present, to covers of *Hello* in a waiting room, and a white-jacketed man 'scanning penumbras on illuminated screens'. This shoring up of history around the contemporary moment features across O'Mahony's work, with the past as a body of water that continuously ebbs and flows around the present. She uses this strategy to make a scathing social observation in 'O'Leary's Grave', contrasting the re-make of The Rising in Collins' Barracks with the citizens in Croppy's Acre, 'bedding down there, sharing / sleeping bags and needles, / messing up the view'.

On a more intimate scale, in 'The King of Britain's Daughter', O'Mahony's vision of love involves turning away from 'watching skies / for starlings from home', and finding a landing place where the couple can ...

> ... both walk the strand,
> beach-comb, pick up messages
> they encode for each other.
> Does it matter what bird says your name,
> or which coast it flies from?

Throughout poems that explore relationships, nature, commemoration, and the hidden histories in the landscape, O'Mahony undercuts her own capacity for beautiful language with the determinedly 'unpoetic'. In 'A Poppy for Aoife', for example, the luscious image of 'each green pod plumped / and split its seams / letting red silk out', is countered by the everyday 'slow-mo reveal'. '"In Ainm Croim"' plants a 'linguistic stick of rock' in a poem about deep family roots. This strategy keeps the poet's own tone of voice front and centre, anchoring the reader through the explorations of landscape and historical memory. 'Do Not Ask' and 'The Hare on the Chest' are wonderfully intimate memorials, the latter having a quiet wit and wonderful symmetry, as well as catching the reader up in the drama of the hare's 'desperate leap of faith into the dark / gap between the man's coat and chest'.

The short series of 'Hollow Woman' poems charts the experience of illness and diagnosis, creating images of anxious waiting, of 'old news is better / than new news / when you have to wait / in a room with four doors, / none of them open, yet' ('The Hollow Woman Waits'). In 'The Hollow Woman on the Island', the sea stands for the unknown future; the woman watches it 'lick its lips / at the edge of the pier', and dreams it will draw her in 'till she's smooth, buffed', to be picked up and 'pocketed, placed with care / on a mantlepiece, a grave-top'. These poems of individual vulnerability frame the remainder of the collection, which explores the interweaving of faith and family (in 'Mantra', 'At Masada', and 'Holy Land'), as well as individual poems such as 'Orphan', which contrasts 'home' and 'the home', and powerfully maps dark aspects of Irish social history. Throughout this assured collection, O'Mahony captures the deep pleasure of the natural world, so absorbing it can make one 'forgetful for once / of the rogue cells/ multiplying' ('The Hollow Woman Reflects on the Illusion of Abundance'). In 'Super Moon on the M6', the moon is described as 'rising / like a parachute in reverse', a 'disc so bright / it made me laugh out loud / when I recognised her'. In 'Absence', she remembers where 'swifts carved their curve', and in 'Two Encounters with the *Lutra lutra*', she cautions herself on glimpsing an otter in the river Dodder: 'we fumble with ways / not to forget. *Just watch.*'

In an echo of *The Built Moment*'s penultimate poem, O'Mahony also closes her collection with an meditation on sea and faith, remarking in 'If Homer Came to Iveragh ...', that 'prayer starts / in the same place as story: / where the mind stills long enough / to hear sea crashing on rock'; and ending with the resonant image of a story that 'starts / where each knot of barbed wire / links phrase to phrase, / chair to chair of the listeners / circled in rooms, round fires / gazing at the face of the teller'.

Mary O'Donnell

MY MOTHER REMEMBERS HER IRISH

Like Alice, she has fallen down the rabbit hole.
In a room at the bottom,

rejecting a bottle labelled DRINK ME,
she reaches for the cracked urn of language:

SPEAK ME, it invites.
White hair in disarray, she unstops it.

The contents fizz up and over the lip of glaze
as she recovers the sounds she forgot

after schooling. Now, she has broken away
from the language bunker,

its torqued English,
takes to speech at the midnight hour.

As if fighting the Jabberwocky,
she uses old songs to push against a paralysis

of chair-lifts, walking frames,
they emerge on her tongue, ancient oratorio:

síolta; beidh aonach amárach; cad dúirt tú,
a chailín álainn? Ba mhaith liom dul abhaile.

Such softness that rarely found its way in English,
now honeys her tongue in the magical flight of dotage.

Time, released, enriches conversation.
"Did you know that this Republic was born

70 years ago today? Years after the Maglioccos
in the town taught me Mussolini's anthem."

We speak of Easter music, the St. Matthew Passion,
her *ceol cráifeach*. She wonders

if the sun will dance, Easter Sunday morning,
on the hill above her house at Kilnadrain,

where she wants to return sometime soon.
        Mo thinteán féin, she adds.

Nathan Fidler

HAY FEVER

Rubbery fingertips poke
at sore, damp eyes.

In the back of my throat
where my body tries

desperately to drown
the pollen at my expense,

I can taste the medicine;
glassy, creamy, separated

from itself. The dark bottle
sits in the kitchen, snugly

waiting on a shelf for morning,
noon and night.

I let my eyes bulge and
friends steal glances at me

in assembly, whispering,
wishing they had not thrown

freshly cut grass.

Maureen Gallagher

ELEGY FOR A GOOD MOTHER

You'll never again bite into a blackberry,
Taste its sweet juice,
Grind seeds in your teeth.

Never again look out to the lake
Where moorhens dip, nor watch
The coots with their nuns' coifs.

Nor will you walk the high road,
Name a flower in every front –
A wonder to its Latin root.

And still the briars insist,
Thrust out, filling space,
Still the water ripples.

And your lovely image lingers
In the house where you raised a family,
The garden flush with hollyhock.

You are woven into this townland,
On rambling rose and hawthorn,
Honeysuckle, meadowsweet.

Sandra Yannone

GRATITUDE WORKSHOP
NOTEBOOK #12, 1991

– for Lucie Brock-Broido (1956–2018)

She said, *Poetry is about demons*
and *to trust the interior of ice.*

I ruminate over all the advice
we must endure in this world,

a precarious stack of dishes
at the edge of the sink

or a game of midnight freeze tag
in a field of no moon.

She said, *Don't apologize. Don't explain.*
If fourteen fish swim past

what does the fifteenth look like?
The darkest hour of the recurring bruise.

She said, *Court tension*
and risk. They don't exchange

names. They don't even shake
greasy hands. About doubt?

It's terminal, more than a blessing.
Forgiveness is another night of testimony.

How is it you remain unmarried?
I told myself it was the mattress.

I had a bed. I did not lie.
I find fire delectable and can sleep.

She said, *Be careful not to be*
too good, so I pretend

to fidget with some anger.
In simplicity, the simple.

Let the day bear out
its breakdown of horoscopes

like coins that disappear
into the glass face of a parking meter.

All description must be revelation.
I can forgive only the first grey hair.

And in response to my longing,
I burn the toast.

Deirdre Cartmill

TORN

I see you crying at the gate,
and I am back at another gate

where you hoisted me on your shoulders

and the horn of the hunt
quivered through the fields,

and I saw the horses race
but I didn't see the hare,

blood pulsing

as its hind legs flexed
to bolt, zigzag, leap,

and I didn't see the hounds' teeth
rip into its neck,

then trail its dripping entrails

back to their masters
to blood their young,

and as I watch you weep
I still don't see

what lies beneath the hedge line,

– the blood stains on your shirt,
the debris on your tongue,

because I didn't see what you saw,
the ripped limbs flung across the street,

the dead eyes open,

and the wee one floating in the water
in a torn green blanket.

Seán Hewitt

DOUBLE POSITIVE

Vona Groarke, *Double Negative* (The Gallery Press, 2019), €11.95.
Frank McGuinness, *The Wedding Breakfast* (The Gallery Press, 2019), €11.95.

There is something of Rachel Boast, and of WS Graham, in the
philosophical conundrums of *Double Negative*, and in Groarke's slantwise
gaze. *Double Negative* explores ageing, loneliness, monotony, but with a
sharp and considered wit. The collection is threaded with a series of
poems written 'against' concepts: 'Against Harm'; 'Against Loss'; 'Against
Age'. In many of these poems, as in 'Against Darkness', the speaker turns
time over on itself, a sort of optical volta that twists perspective and
inverts the vision:

> In the museum of the photographer's studio
> I find I cannot breathe.
> The room is light-tight, clogged
> and hellish, this stepping around the props
> and costumes and lamps and cameras.
> There are too many of us.
>
> The photo of the little boy
> has a toy horse in it and, yes,
> here is that horse six decades on
> only this time I am the little boy
> perched and primed for the record now
> and we all know what happened to him.

These are poems that undo their own certainties, unravel their knots, slip
the ground from under us. Their tone is usually measured, demonstrative,
but this suggests a stability that the poems themselves shirk.

In 'This Poem', Groarke plays with potential and meaning, with trans-
parency. 'This is the poem that won't open / no matter where you press.'
And later, 'This poem has no big plans for you / which is something, as
poems go.' The poem is allowed to be, to exist in a freer and less circum-
scribed place. The voice is often nonchalant, apparently uninterested in
the reader. 'Whimsy? Perhaps. Or metaphor. / You choose. / I'm afraid
I can't help you with that' ('Against Boredom'). But such presentation,
in suggesting that the poem might be an opaque surface, and difficult to
penetrate, does not do justice to the skill with which Groarke opens up
language, and the spaces of the poem.

These poems are deconstructive in intent, and demonstrative in their approach. Often, the titles offer a key to the poems, sitting in a meta-phorical relation to them whilst simultaneously critiquing the possibility of metaphor itself. In 'What It Feels Like Is No Way The Same As How It Feels', Groarke gets right into the gaps of poetry, peering inside, quite miraculously opening up – if only for a split-second – whatever it is that exists outside the game of language.

There is an aural delicacy, too, which is intricate and unobtrusive. Groarke's rhymes are subtle, often half-rhymes and echoes, as in the opening stanza of 'Against Monotony':

> Today, a two-hundred mile drive and nothing
> at the end of it but a glass of Merlot
> and a radio fugue for voice and clarinet
> which is a lot, when you think about it.

In many ways, the poems here are kaleidoscopic, revealing new angles and surfaces as their subjects are considered, and moved into new arrangements. If there are some poems that are a little less convincing, a little less taut (as in 'Poem with My Mother and Frank O'Hara'), the overall quality of the book is beyond doubt. In this, her seventh collection, Vona Groarke shows herself to be a poet of delicate craft and daring insight, working at the height of her powers.

Launched alongside Groarke's *Double Negative* at a Poetry Ireland event this summer, Frank McGuinness's *The Wedding Breakfast*, his sixth collection, opens with a photograph taken in Buncrana, Co Donegal. In it, his grandmother and neighbours are standing in an otherwise empty street, by a gateway. The caption tells us that 'the gateway leads to my grandfather's forge over which I was born'. In that vein, this latest collec-tion dives into history, both personal and national. Some of the poems here are small – songs, or progressions of imagistic stanzas – while others are discursive, combining the casual with the philosophically ambitious.

In the shorter, less narrative poems, such as 'Knights', 'Tullydish', 'The Bay Tree', and 'Apples', McGuinness's imagery is more unexpected, and there is a grace to the rhythms that is missing in the poems with less measured stanzas. In these more sparse poems, there is just enough room for mystery, and for the reader's involvement. The images have some-thing of the archetype, something almost Yeatsian: 'I came across three birds in flight, / a pike and lances singing, / illusions of fife and drum, / the rising moon of morning' ('Knights'). Some of the best poems in the collection are elegies. 'The Grave', a poem in two parts, is haunting in its images – 'The garden sang songs each New Year's Eve'. The final elegiac poem, 'Who Could Survive the Atlantic Ocean', is ceremonious and heartfelt.

As in Groarke's *Double Negative*, the tone here is often declarative, and ageing is a prominent concern. McGuinness's rhymes, too, are often subtle, and his poems can be circular, turning back to their own beginnings to measure a progress, or lack thereof. In 'Orion', for example, a father and son change places:

> When my father muddled himself
> with Orion the hunter
> he chased fantastic prey
> through strange Inishowen,
> urging on his bread van
> along the limb of the sun,
> steering as if the stars
> were earth beneath our feet.
>
> These feet, these stars,
> they were our guide.
> I fill his shoes now
> with the dust of our days,
> seeing him ascend
> leaving us behind,
> implacable and cold.
> He is hungry Orion.

The rhymes are subtle, and this gives a sense of structure that the language otherwise lacks metrically. The progression of the images is less surprising than in Groarke, as is the perspective.

Overall, this reflects a less acute gaze in *The Wedding Breakfast*. In the title poem, for example, the surgeon 'was Greek, some Apollo. / He fancied himself another Dylan, / blood on the tracks like blood on the lancet.' The associations here seem a little odd, or obvious. That is not to say that, on the broader level, the poems in McGuinness's collection do not attain an impressive scope – in 'The Wedding Breakfast' alone, we move from the Royal Victoria Hospital, Belfast, to some striking imagery in 'gifts of cats' tails and egg shells', through Chinatown, Soho, and on to an affair in Dublin. McGuinness weaves these strands with skill and craft, showing a confidence in the ability of his poems to shift and move between ideas. Though the images themselves might not always surprise us, the narrative movements of the poems often do.

Mary Montague

REQUIEM

The sound is of distance; of low-tide breakers
collapsing onto a vast plain of spray-gauzed sand;
of a salt wind's sting. 'You never know when
it's the last time.' That day, I did. Or knew
its likelihood. It was a summer-bright September
afternoon and I had managed to prise my parents out
of their house of decay and despair – goading
my father with something close to those very words.

And my father responded: rising for me, I see now,
when he would rise for no-one. Miraculously,
it felt then, he materialised, fully-dressed, in the hall.
I had already folded my mother into the front seat,
had called our goodbyes, was about to pull the door
behind me. So there were the perennial
disruptive rearrangements: her into the back,
while he waited in dishevelled imperious dignity.

I don't remember the specifics of that journey
but it's easy to call up the inevitable spats
over smoking in the car; the pointed remarks
about my driving; the way my mother's eyes
closed in the mirror. And the nerve-wracking
toilet-stops, me, with one clutched on each arm,
steering our path before casting off, fingers
crossed, my father alone into the gents.

Adrift of the cliffs' massed reproach,
I pulled the car up. The beach was the same
breathless expanse, primary colours, exulting waves.
My mother refused her opened door,
but he, grimly shaking me off, leaned
into his riven stare and embarked across
the wind-scathed waste – who knows
whether to beg or dare its desert to take him.

Goggled by thick glasses, beggared by ash-dusted
clothes grown too large, for a few minutes
my father banished his decrepit shuffle
to stride across Rossnowlagh Strand
in sunshine. I followed, off side, well behind,
carrying all the summer days, as people
swung wide of him, this crazy horse,
bit between his teeth, just off the lunge.

I judged enough and well enough when I headed
him off for him to agree: the last march was done.
He'd breath left to lurch his way back. We took it slowly,
each pause a ruse, but some of the light's brilliance,
the ocean's bleach and scour, wet sand near-white
with gleam, could have glinted through diabetes-blurred
sight; tarred lungs might have breathed more freely
to ease an infarcted heart. We said nothing.

My gnomed mother peered from the depths
of the back seat. My father clambered
into the front, leaving me to look around,
gather up, in his stead. The windscreen cased
his blanched face and dust-vague expression.
Was he just sinking back into his hollow,
his eyes fresh-glazed by the wind's salt?
His forehead ruckled. He looked away.

I'm left to trail his final pilgrimage. I have no
Damascene insight from witnessing the forcing
of a frail body, a broken mind, to an old obedience.
Except for this: that there is an almost-holiness
in that defiance. Memory thrashes. I shy from it.
But if my father's soul dwells somewhere,
let it be a fine Rossnowlagh day; where he strides;
then he rests; and then we walk

Ger Feeney

A SMART BOLLIX

I have detected
From time to time
More the odd time
Than all the time
A certain reluctance
Amongst sixty-four-year-olds
Wearing matching
Boiler suits
And toolboxes

To giving up
Their seat on the 130
From Lower Abbey Street
To Castle Avenue
To fifty-year-old pensioners

Fuck off ya smart bollix
Said one sixty-four-year-old
Wearing matching
Boiler suit
And toolbox
Completely oblivious
To the fact
That being a
Smart enough bollix
To be a pensioner
At fifty was
Neither here nor there

Ivy Bannister

MATERNITY 1924

– for J.E.S.

You do know I tried
to get rid of her?

Scratch of a match.
The suck of breath
as Ma draws in smoke.
Under the table it's lady legs and me.
The toes of Ma's shoes tap.
Missus Bishop's trotters
are stuffed into slippers.

It was near on a bottle I drank,
gin, pure gin, that scorched
mouth, throat and gullet,
certain to burn it out, but
to be sure I jumped
off this table for an hour.

There's smells of butter, cinnamon
and toast, as well as Ma's smoke.
Missus Bishop's teeth clatter.
She coughs, crumbs scatter.
There's a rip in the lino.
Underneath, a spider.
It looks at me and I look at it.

I tell you that night my head
was a whirl of pinks and oranges
when I tumbled into bed,
I was that sure
there'd be blood by morning.
As you see, there was not.

Under the table, my legs tuck up.
Arms cross over my chest.

Aoife Lyall

MONTH'S MIND

We don't know which ones we're meant to bring
so we settle on the yellows for all the sorrys
there are. We pick the smallest bunch. Full
of buds, but no flowers, we lay them to rest
in the river. Our slow footsteps mourning the dying
shadows, we walk back to the house, together

and alone. Once home, we bury our good shoes
at the bottom of the wardrobe. We pour the tea
and unwrap plates of sandwiches and cake.
In low voices we talk a little about the life
you never lived, and the house you never lived in
is overwhelmed by all the people who didn't know to come.

Jessica Traynor

WIDE ANGLE / CLOSE UP

Maureen Boyle, *The Work of a Winter* (Arlen House, 2018), €13.
Ciarán O'Rourke, *The Buried Breath* (The Irish Pages Press, 2018), £18 hb.
Eithne Lannon, *Earth Music* (Turas Press, 2019), €12.

The title of Maureen Boyle's *The Work of a Winter* refers to more than
just the book's eponymous poem sequence. These are poems which have
been painstakingly crafted over time. There is nothing hurried here; in
their intricacy, these poems demand a reader's careful attention, offering
much reward in return. In 'Incunabula', a deceptively taut sequence
recalling a family history by turns poignant and charming, the poet roots
us firmly in the Northern milieu of her upbringing. Observations on
grief and attitudes to women are captured with particular insight, with
the blame over a child's death carelessly attributed:

> ... It took years for her to tell of this and the
> months that would pass in the high house that should
> have held a baby – my aunt brutal in accusation
> that walking to her mother's in the village was to blame.

In a winter-themed collection, fireside tales abound, and Boyle gives
voice to a number of protagonists, demonstrating the dramatic potential
of poetry; how the excavation of trauma is not solely the preserve of the
confessional poet. Boyle clearly feels a duty of care towards these voices.
Stand-out poems include 'The Witch in the Wall', with its earthy surrealism,
and 'Weather Vane', a deeply empathetic act of ventriloquism which
recalls a pregnant woman incarcerated in a convent, cleaning roof slates
as a punishment:

> I talk to my baby up here.
> We're not supposed to but the wind
> takes the words away.

The collection ranges widely in its subject-matter, from childhood
memories to Irish history, to the legacies of Irish educators abroad in the
form of the titular sequence, which addresses the work of Mícheál Ó
Cléirigh, chief compiler of the *Annals of the Four Masters*. Through
the use of a number of sequences, Boyle creates a through-line whose
sinuous movement fittingly invokes the knot-work illuminations in a
manuscript. In the final section of this sequence, the culmination of this
ambitious historical project takes on a transcendent note:

A flock of great white butterflies bedding down
to winter in the walls had mistaken the heat of our fire
for an early spring and come back to life too soon.
No angels then, but marvellous still. Is that what death
will be, I wonder, a gentle waking into the warmth of
God?

This collection marks the debut of a talented writer who has spent time
honing their craft. It will be interesting to see if Boyle's next collection
retains *The Work of a Winter*'s wide-ranging, panoramic approach, or
perhaps chooses to 'zoom in'. The more closely-themed work in this
collection suggests the latter also lies within Boyle's abilities, and it will
be interesting to see what challenges she sets herself next.

In a generation of young poets with a marked preference for academic
archness and high/low culture mash-ups, Ciarán O'Rourke blazes a
singular trail. *The Buried Breath*, one of the first collections published by
The Irish Pages Press, is a debut demonstrating a social conscience and
a sustained engagement with world literature. From the striking cover
image of migrants struggling on a foundering boat to O'Rourke's series
of responses to figures such as Miklós Radnóti, alongside his energetic
and fluent translations of Catullus, this is a collection which merges an
eclectic range of interests. In 'Postcards from Palestine', the challenging
task of giving voice to a war-torn nation is achieved through a poem
which builds in intensity through four sections to an impassioned plea for
empathy:

Remember my words,
as if they were warmed by the blood in my wrist,
as if they were cut from the coil of my tongue.

The task of weaving these strands together is achieved through O'Rourke's
strong instinct for metre and rhythm, favouring regularly stressed short-
lined tercets which lend the poems a strong musicality. They also allow
little room for indulgence of any kind, leading to a singular kind of clean-
boned poem; strong at the core yet delicately rendered, with lines such as
'History is one / disaster , feeding / off another, or: // what poems are
made / to witness/ and withstand', from 'The Killing March', arresting
the reader with their elegant directness. If the choice of this form married
with the typographical choices occasionally leads to a relatively brief
poem feeling rather drawn out over a number of pages, the freshness of
the language keeps the reader engaged, as in 'Guatemala, 1967', a poem
in memory of Otto René Castillo, which begins with the memorable
lines:

Say nation
and the deer and moon
unlatch a shadow;

the darkness
quickens;
a candle blows.

O'Rourke's translations and 'variations' warrant special mention as an exercise which may seem unusual for a debut author, but here these intimate engagements with poets both ancient and modern allow O'Rourke room to flex creative muscles within set forms, leading to an intriguing merging of the poet's singular style with that of his forebears. This series culminates in O'Rourke's own poem to Catullus; an invigorating torrent of language:

Catullus, dawn-young and delicate as rain,
I thank a thousand gods I never met you.
For days you've lingered, brazen on the corners,
hot-fingering your puny cock, screaming love
to some piss-pale heaven, under which love poems
burst impossibly from life-embezzled beds.

A poet who approaches both the ancient and the modern with the same insight and sensitivity, O'Rourke surely has a long and distinguished poetic career ahead.

By contrast to the wide-angle lens through which the previous two poets view the world, Eithne Lannon's debut *Earth Music* is concerned with a more private universe, where her miniaturist's sensibility can illuminate a series of epiphanic moments. This is a collection which revels in language and its ability to render the everyday beautiful. Rather than engaging in the narrative tradition, these poems are word-pictures or captured moments of reflection. In 'Enough', the first poem in the collection, we encounter Lannon in meditative mood, eager to capture a moment of transformation, where 'currents below' ...

carry on their secret life, ruffling
wavelets to a sandy paste,

lifting bubble-scuff to a frothy spin
of airborne river breath,

and the moment of a life
that stays with itself

in that moment, is surely
enough.

A kind of manifesto for what follows, the language here is luminous,
vivid, full of fresh and surprising imagery which immerses the reader in
the poem's moment. North Co Dublin – Loughshinny in particular – is
rendered as a living presence in poems such as 'Loughshinny Bay' and
'Loughshinny Trilogy'; the latter poem delves into stories of the locale in
a rush of vivid, musical language which breathes life into the bay's
history, lending past events a tangible urgency:

and they say death by drowning is simple,
like a silk cloth gliding to the ocean floor—

these men were desperate, their fear lunging
from the frantic yawl to the dense harbour wall

and no one can reach them.

At times, the close focus on language and beauty mean that the reader
might miss the grit at the poem's heart; that concrete happening which
sparks the poem and tethers it to the world of the real. Poems such as
'On Millennium Bridge' and 'May 28th' strike closer to the heart, the
concrete details of the real world puncturing the beauty of the poems to
create intriguing juxtapositions. 'Before my sister's death' introduces a
directness of tone, while maintaining the delicate, almost surreal lyricism
common throughout the poems here:

I stepped suddenly
into the clear halo of her eyes,

their blue light inscribed with endings,
the recent cold of her future

carved into its edges, colour stretched
to the brink of where darkness begins.

Here, the marriage of the concrete and the conceptual anchors the poem
emotionally for the reader. Lannon is a poet of great linguistic facility,
whose work is suffused with the numinous.

Jean Riley

OUT OF HERE

You hear it, his holler. See arms flail
like wings, the fold, stretch of his limbs
like a hare running, his urge to escape.
Gone with his fear, we're left in its wake.

We spend the day hip-to-hip, exclaim
at daddy-long-legs coming and going,
at ash-keys twirling, and we name things,
cats beech-nuts bats ...

I riddle the stove, haul a kettle to pour
your bath. As it cools, sunset illumines
our windows and woods, our faces;
till it drains, leaves us a quiet gloom

to make light of. Tilley lamps, brighten.
You whoop and flex your piston limbs
to splash and power your boat – will it
get us out?

Slippery-smooth, towel-swaddled, drowsy
in Viyella, you're nearly there. I lean
to lay you down – you won't let go.
(I must get you away, tomorrow).

He's quiet when he comes in, late.
In the morning, feeds cats, brings wood,
makes tea.
                    Makes you smile.

Colette Tennant

THE DAUGHTER I DIDN'T HAVE

I.

If I had two daughters –
would it be hard not to love one more than the other?

The one with the vulnerable chin,
the one with the darker hair?

Would I teach my baby daughter the names of the stars,
and her sister only the phases of the moon?

Would my new daughter and I sit at our Baldwin upright
playing duets for hours?

Maybe old hymns and I'd let her
have the melody every time.

If I had another daughter, we'd
name all the birds we could see from her bedroom window.

We'd hold hands at Riverfront Park.
We'd find the osprey nest but never tell.

II.

What if my unbegotten daughter
grew up and became a showgirl in Las Vegas?

What if she dressed like an almost-bare angel
and posed on Las Vegas Boulevard with anyone who asked?

Her white flare on the Bellagio sidewalk,
the length of her lit every time the fountains danced.

It would be almost Biblical
except for placard-carrying prophets

spouting into the night
a litany of punishments through their wireless mics.

If her tourists would ask her,
my almost-angel daughter would offer them a blessing.

Instead, they just stand speechless,
hugging each other,

smiling into a sudden burst of light.

Luke Morgan

REFURBISHMENT

They told me it would look like this
and frankly, I didn't believe them.
How could I, when scaffolding
held up the arches
and the sharp buzzing of distant machines
in echoed chambers
was like your voice downstairs,
asking if I wanted anything from Londis.

Now, everything is colour-coordinated,
the ceiling is vaulted
and it does me good to walk around
on carpets that make you forget
you're standing on pure granite.
The stained-glass window in the lobby
gives off its delusion of light.
I remember when its ledge
was filled with dust
that dropped from the ceiling,
the sort that would dance
above your unmade bed on mornings
months ago, while I sat on the edge of it
listening to you sing in the shower.

Nicola Geddes

FIND TWO STONES
TAP GENTLY TOGETHER
IN EQUAL PULSES
THREE TIMES

Under the bare bones of a birch in winter
I found two stones, tapped them gently together

by a buckled hawthorn, gale-grown, white petal blown
under the ruby crown of September's rowan
I tapped and tapped a century-long song

between Ben Mhór and Ben Choanaigh
a hard hot sun, a near-dry river
I find two stones, tap them together
the echo returns the mountains' answer

found within sound of stone on stone
is the breath of all that has been and gone
and here, in my hands, are the trees and the weather
the rhythm of land and the pulse of forever.

Author's note: The project *Find Two Stones*, upon which this recent
poem is based, began in 1979 and will run until 2079. Stone tapping 'is
a musical composition in which you can participate anytime', but with
'crescendo dates' marked out throughout the century, where people all
over the world connect in this simple act. For further information, visit
this facebook page: www.facebook.com/groups/findtwostones

Morag Smith

NEVERTHELESS

You turn the heating down and open windows
steal the quilt and snore at four a.m.
you watch *Star Trek*, claim fluency in Klingon
but

my habits like my politics are lazy
the dust lies thick, perhaps we should become
High Achievers, taking back control
but

our grass is knee high, full of weeds and daisies
triffid contradictions thrive and bloom
one day it may finally engulf us
but

you are the conjunct of my conjunction
the impossibility of anything
other than this declaration – no ifs
or buts

Ailbhe Barrett
Saplings, 2017
Aquatint, etching
20 x 18 cm

Ailbhe Barrett
Kilmore (detail), 2017
Etching with monoprint
49.5 x 70 cm

Ailbhe Barrett
Rebound (Sycamores), 2018
Etching
18 x 24 cm

Ailbhe Barrett
Morning, Doorlus (iii), 2016
Etching
17 x 23 cm

Ailbhe Barrett
Doorlus (iv), 2018
Oil on canvas
105 x 72 cm

www.ailbhebarrett.com

Ciarán O'Rourke

'MADMAN, CLOWN – SUCCESS': WILLIAM CARLOS WILLIAMS IN
IRELAND

Recalling his fondness as a young poet for 'rising rhythm, falling rhythm,
[and metric] feet with Greek names', in 1961 the celebrated writer, Robert
Lowell, concluded of his early, Pulitzer Prize-winning work: 'Everything
I did was grand, ungrammatical, and had a timeless, hackneyed quality.'
But '[a]ll this was ended', Lowell wrote, 'by reading Williams', a figure
whose vernacular verse and roots-up depictions of daily American life
changed what the younger writer imagined to be possible (and acceptable)
in the art, 'as though some homemade ship, part Spanish galleon, part
paddle-wheels, kitchen pots, and elastic bands and worked by hand, had
anchored to a filling station.'

In its largeness, ease, and exaggerated invention, the image is unforgettable;
but also helpful in indicating both the nature and scale of the influence
that the older poet exerted on writers of Lowell's generation, and others
later. From the 1910s onwards, as prevailing literary appetites seemed to
be for either artful pentameters or abstruse experimentalism, Williams
pioneered a speech-based poetry of precise social observation, a poetry
grounded in the specificities of his locale in Rutherford, New Jersey, and
in his own manifold experiences as a paediatrician and doctor-on-call,
serving largely working-class families in the surrounding area. 'They call
me and I go', Williams wrote in 1921, on 'a frozen road / past midnight,
a dust / of snow caught / in the rigid wheeltracks', to attend to a patient
'laboring / to give birth to / a tenth child'. Like much of Williams's work,
the poem is stripped to its essentials and clear in its social understanding
of the scene described, offering a delicately cadenced, disarmingly plain-
spoken record of things as they are. While contemporaries like TS Eliot
and Ezra Pound were forging fractured meditations on the losses of
modernity – allusion-heavy and Euro-centric – Williams's home-grown
modernism sought to document and reflect the realities of life in America,
providing what he called 'a recognisable image' of his place and moment,
in a language accessible to all. 'What good is it to me', Williams queried,
'if you can't understand it?'

Although Williams famously had to self-publish his first five collections
of poetry due to a lack of editorial interest in his work, in his later years
(and posthumously) he came to be regarded as one of the most original
American poets of the twentieth century. 'One is', if anything, 'rather
embarrassed at the necessity of calling Williams original', the poet and

critic Randall Jarrell once noted, for 'it is like saying that a Cheshire Cat smiles.' Part of the reason, no doubt, that writers as stylistically far-flung as Elizabeth Bishop and Allen Ginsberg, Frank O'Hara and Denise Levertov, later cited the importance of the 'American English' register, egalitarian outlook, and insistent contemporaneity of Williams's work to their own development. Even beyond the hallowed halls of American verse, Williams's reputation has cast a long and bright-spangled shadow, encompassing composer Steven Reich's absorbing musical rendition of his mid-century poetry collection, *The Desert Music*, and film director Jim Jarmusch's tribute – with a dose of slapstuck humour and a permeating attentiveness to the rhythms of place – to Williams's poem, *Paterson*, in the 2016 film of that title. Like his famous 'red wheel / barrow' and the icebox plums 'so sweet / and so cold', Williams's cultural presence has become, apparently, ubiquitous.

Less remarked upon, however, are the links between the work of this now-acclaimed American poet and that of an array of Irish writers across the twentieth century. Although having no ancestral connections to Ireland (his parents, English and half-Basque originally, transplanted themselves from Puerto Rico to New Jersey before he was born), Williams throughout his life was forthright in his admiration of what he perceived as Ireland's creation of 'an indigenous art' based on local conditions and concerns – and one which he felt American moderns could learn from. Williams went so far as to have the characters of his play, *A September Afternoon*, set during the American revolution, speak in the same drawn-out dialect exemplified in the works of JM Synge, which had emerged on the radar of avant-garde circles in New York. 'It's this we've been fearing the two weeks now they've been camping beyond the hills,' one character intones – with an idiomatic emphasis (or over-emphasis) worthy even of WB Yeats's Hibernicised dramatic productions.

Williams in fact met Yeats in person while on a visit to Paris in 1924, recalling his arrival at a much-frequented studio to find the Irish figure 'in a darkened room [...] reading by candlelight' from a series of (quite conventional) verses by the New Zealand poet, Ernest Dowson, surrounded by a 'very small gathering of his protégés, maybe five or six young men and women, members of the Abbey Theatre group.' Williams's portrait of the eminent litterateur is of course as amusing as it is atmospheric, Yeats's 'beautiful voice' deepening to convey the supposed intensities of Dowson's poetry – which, Williams says flatly, 'was not my dish'.

Williams's verdict on Yeats's own work, however, was a different matter. Writing in 1913 to Harriet Monroe, editor of *Poetry* magazine, Williams credits his own urge to modernise and break free from the 'fixed iambic measure' of traditional Anglophone verse to Yeats's example: 'he teaches what can be done with the three-syllable foot', Williams observes with an earnest exactitude, 'by dropping the last syllable in the foot every time but once or twice in the entire poem', and so clears the way for 'some other kind of measure' to be worked out by future versifiers. Yeats may never quite have seen 'the figure 5 / in gold / on a red / firetruck' the way Williams did – the world-in-motion passing, bit by bit, into line-broken revelation – but his impulse to combine lyric art with regional speech and preoccupations (in Ireland) nonetheless proved serviceable to this relatively unknown doctor-poet's efforts to develop a new understanding of literary craft and purpose.

Many years later, in 1949 – and in the wake of the anthology, *1000 Years of Irish Poetry*, edited by his friend and frequent literary typist, Kitty Hoagland – Williams revisited and confirmed the importance of Yeats as a creative influence, penning a poem he called, resonantly, 'Cuchulain'. Whereas in Yeats's 'Cuchulain Comforted', the 'Violent and famous' warrior takes his place in the underworld among 'Convicted cowards all, by kindred slain', Williams's hero retains his social stature, albeit as seen by his once-lover, Aife, who has been left behind. 'His life lived in / me warmed / at his fires // A power in the night', the poem reads, Cuchulain's reputation near the end of his days coming strangely to resemble Yeats's own: 'Mad-man, clown – success'. 'Mad Ireland' may have hurt Yeats 'into poetry', as WH Auden perceived a decade earlier, but his 'gift' and legacy 'survived it all' – a perspective on their shared literary forebear that Williams seems also to have held.

1949 also marked the moment when Williams's only Irish-published poem was printed – in the October issue of *Poetry Ireland*, edited by David Marcus. Entitled 'May 1st Tomorrow', the poem is a playful exercise in free association and a self-satirising account of literary labour and its trials. 'The mind's a queer sponge', Williams writes, 'squeeze it and out come bird songs' – a proposition that recurs, ironically, later in the piece as a pure interruption of the 'view of the mind / that, in a way gives milk' to the thirsting poet: '*Chuck, chuck, chuck. Toe whee. Chuck!*' With linguistic verve and exuberant self-satisfaction, the poem both enacts and mocks the process of its own composition – a reminder of Williams's own experimental tendencies.

Similar procedures are found throughout the epic poem, *Paterson* (if on a larger and more complex scale), the early sections of which Williams also completed and published in these years. Described by Lowell as an attempt to represent 'Whitman's America' in modern times, 'grown pathetic and tragic, brutalized by inequality, disorganised by industrial chaos, and faced with annihilation', the poem sets out 'to form the colors' of such a vista 'in the terms of some / back street', finding in the 'poor, the invisible, thrashing, breeding / debased city' of its title a vision of social and cultural renewal. The poem thus delves into the history, geography, and many voices of its locale, in an emblematic effort to discover the often gruelling, if sometimes delectable realities that undergird American life mid-way through the twentieth century. It stands – as Lowell and many others have contended – as a 'great American poem.' And in terms of structure and technique, among its most important influences were the novels of James Joyce.

As before with Yeats, Williams met and dined with Joyce while holidaying in Paris in the 1920s, remembering in his *Autobiography* the Irish writer's 'small, compressed head, straight nose and no lips'; that he 'spoke with a distinct, if internationalized, Irish accent'; and that he 'would take no hard liquor, only white wine'. Entertaining as such reminiscences are, the encounter of the two men was perhaps less creatively formative than Williams's self-immersion in Joyce's work. Before writing *Paterson* 'I had been reading *Ulysses*', Williams remarks in 1958, and was 'influenced [by] Joyce who had made Dublin the hero of his book' – a book that seemed to allow the American poet in turn '[to fall] in love with my city'.

It's a theme that resurfaces throughout Williams's essays and letters: in his desire to create an art responsive to the actualities of life in contemporary America, he turns to Joyce's works for guidance. We find Williams in 1927, for example, commending the manner in which 'Joyce's style' seems to bend and shapeshift to reflect 'the facts' of urban Dublin, his apparent artfulness arising from 'the realistic conditions that compel him' – an insight prefiguring one of the fundamental assertions of Williams's own literary practice: that there can be (as he phrases it in *Paterson*) 'No ideas but / in the facts'.

In the same period, during the initial serialisation of Joyce's *Work in Progress* (later *Finnegans Wake*) in *transition* magazine, Williams placed himself at the forefront of critical debates concerning the new work – to the extent, indeed, that he was included, along with Thomas MacGreevy and one Samuel Beckett, among twelve contributors to the first ever roundtable collection of essays elucidating and defending Joyce's literary achievements, '*Our exagmination round his factification for incamination of work in progress*'. Joyce's next book will be nothing less than 'the leap of a new force', Williams's contribution declares with evident excitement, asserting that it 'is a new literature, a new world, that [Joyce] is undertaking' – proof, perhaps, of his own thoroughly modernist belief that by revitalising 'a static, worn out language', the contemporary artist can uncover 'a literary way [to] save the world'. A grand statement, certainly, but one that indicates concisely the esteem, energy, and seemingly effortless understanding with which Williams engaged even the more difficult phases of Joyce's work.

If the modernisms of Joyce and Yeats influenced Williams's poetic development in a variety of ways, there are also some fascinating connections between the American bard and a number of later Irish writers. Eavan Boland once hailed Williams as an 'obstinate, generous titan of demotic verse', while Thomas Kinsella acknowledged his importance in similar terms, writing that the American doctor was instrumental in 'opening up the voice' of the modern poem to the twentieth century at large. Likewise, in the landmark memoir-cum-interview, *Stepping Stones*, Seamus Heaney recalled having 'a short William Carlos Willliamsy line in his ear' while writing his third collection, *Wintering Out* (1972). Intriguingly, both Williams and Heaney wrote poetic responses to PV Glob's images of the preserved, pre-Christian bog body discovered in Denmark in 1950, known as the Tollund Man: Williams in 'A Smiling Dane' (1955) and Heaney in 'The Tollund Man' (1972). Heaney famously took Glob's landmark 1969 compendium, *The Bog People*, as the source text for his poem – as visitors to the National Library of Ireland's *Listen Now Again* exhibition, exploring Heaney's life and work, will learn. Williams, however, was working off near-contemporaneous reports of Glob's findings, and specifically a print and photographic feature on the archaeological dig included in *National Geographic Magazine* (to which he subscribed) in March 1954.

For each writer, the recovered burial victim serves as an icon of ancient atrocity and almost miraculous abidance through time simultaneously, evoking a sensation of alienation mixed with understanding. Although 'Not knowing their tongue', Heaney's piece famously concludes, as a poet familiar with the sectarian conflict of Northern Ireland, 'Out there in Jutland / In the old man-killing parishes / I will feel lost / Unhappy, and at home.' Williams, similarly attuned to the residual intimacy of such violence (although obviously without the same Northern Irish context in mind), in his piece queries:

> And what if
> the image of his frightened executioners
> is not recorded?
> Do we not know

their features

        as if

                it had occurred

today?

            We can still see in his smile

                their grimaces.

In 1955, a year of brutal racist lynchings in the United States – including, notoriously, the murder of fourteen-year-old Emmett Till – Williams's depiction of the exhumed body 'with a rope ... intact / round the neck', along with his grimly ironic imagination of the pre-Christian, tribal executioners by way of the 'features' and 'grimaces' of his fellow citizens, may very well have held a political relatability beyond what he necessarily intended for it. Even without the current of ethical interrogation typi-fied by Heaney's approach, however, Williams's portrait of the 'Smiling Dane' serves as a nuanced affirmation of his adage that '[p]lace is the only universal' – that the particular life of a given scene may generate the frame through which its general meaning billows and enters, as Williams had previously discerned in the work of Yeats and Joyce. 'His stomach', the poem reads,

      its contents examined

              shows him

                        before he died

    to have had

             a meal

                        consisting of local grains

   swallowed whole

            which he probably enjoyed

                though he did not

  much as we do

           chew them.

For Williams, the image of the Tollund Man attains its universality as much through his difference from the present – the swallowing of 'local grains' whole, without chewing them, for example – as through the unsettling familiarity of his features and fate. This, indeed, is the main divergence in the two writers' respective portraits of Glob's bog body: where Heaney sees explicitly delineated in 'his stained face' the 'scattered, ambushed / Flesh of labourers, / Stockinged corpses' of his own land-scape and era, Williams finds 'A Smiling Dane', whose physical frame and bodily habits seem to resist the assimilation into the current moment which they also invite, his excavators deciding in panic to 'quit the place [...] thinking his ghost might walk'.

Also in contrast to Heaney, of course, who in his bog poems was navigating just one turning-point in what would be a much longer poetic trajectory and career, Williams wrote his piece with almost fifty years of literary work behind him – his response to the images of the Tollund Man marking the culmination of a number of well-established creative, formal, and medical concerns. Serving as both a quickened image of the present and a distant fact from the past, Williams's 'Danish native' is (to adapt a line from another of Heaney's poems) 'neither here nor there', but both at once, 'a hurry through which', quite literally, 'known and strange things pass' – to the delight of his beholder, who meets that strangeness not just with the searching vision of a writer, but with the attentive understanding of an anatomist at work.

The point, and the general comparison with Heaney, is hopefully a clarifying one, ultimately bringing us closer to Williams: the New Jersey doctor-poet who was said to have overseen the delivery of 2,000 babies in the Rutherford area over the course of his medical career; and who, when asked in 1954 to name the writers who had most helped his own work to come into the world, included alongside the American 'Whitman' that other indefatigable celebrant of bodies-in-contact and local life, 'James Joyce' – one of the many Irish filling stations at which Williams's home-made ship cast anchor, stopping for fuel.

Doreen Duffy

AN ALTERED LANDSCAPE

They changed the flow
of traffic along the quays
we were seventeen
Bernie Phelan got in a car
with Rasher Mullen
full of the joys of life
We could see her throwing
her head back gurgling, laughing
but he forgot
and drove the wrong way
We could see her head being
flung back
her throat gurgling
Someone made the journey
to our house
to tell us
because we had no phone,
back then

Two days later
we made the trek
to her funeral in Bawnogue
A flat piece of grass
where people dance
that's what Bawnogue means
But there was no dancing that day
We climbed the fence
and crossed the fields
bundles of poppies
splats of red
where the diggers
had thrown them aside
four of us girls
all silent,
when we were never quiet

They've cut the road
straight through there now
so I can hardly remember
the long walk
through the fields of grass
or even where they were
but I remember how
she danced
the night before,
spinning and turning
until
the memory's a blur

John Wedgwood Clarke

FOR SALE

Gulls empty the sky, their squally cries
loosening my hold on things.
Late heat ticks in the tiles and guttering.
The rowan's full breasts shine.
In the attic bedroom, where the wind's
devouring voice in the throat
of the chimney cried out in them,
I've folded up volcanoes, planets,
Kings and Queens of England,
wedged the mobile in the bin,
ending interminable turnings in the internal
thermals, its stored torsions so
nearly time found reversible
before the door slam jumped it crazy.
Blue and white blobs, the cornerstones
of missing stories, diagrams, splotch-beings,
roll to a globe of paint and hair,
a smear of weather. It's too late
to touch-up picked-off wood chip shoals,
herds of animals, hunters, whatever
they saw in them on the edge of sleep.
I stick down the flap of wallpaper
over *I am a person* pencilled on plaster.
Their beds have gone. Only patches remain
where their heads would have been,
precious heads that made this house
flesh-tender, heads tipped back
as they looped arms round our necks
to hold us, books slipping from hands
to thump the floor above us like ripe fruit,
the whole of us listening for the way they turned.

Frank Farrelly

ANOTHER HOME

Roslevin: the huge oak,
sinews tough as rope you'd pull
to moor a masted ship,
the walled garden, the portico,
the wood beside the railway heading west
to Galway and beyond.

Our dog was in her element,
barked with joy until her throat
went silent as the cloud above
the house now was ours.
My father kissed my mother's brow,
her eyes wide, incredulous.

She hugged me to her cotton frock.
I felt the words she burned to say –
knew they were inadequate.
We are here. This is home,
at least until they phoned to say
we have to pack, move again.

Máiríde Woods

THE HOLE IN THE FLOOR

It's still there
despite all the workmen
who have arrived,
promised and left. After
each temporary fix
it bares its grin
a little wider than before.

I'm the one
who's got smaller
frailer, less able
to patch up my argument,
believe in repair,
heave myself up
when grounded.

Despite my pessimism
I'm not totally passive.
I surround it
with wire and plastic,
position chairs, erect
warnings, seek
solutions on Google.

Yet the pesky hole
keeps returning. After
each repair its edges
crumble once more
revealing splodges of damp
in a darkness fertile
with dusty webs.

One day soon, it creaks
you will trip, stumble,
crash definitively
into my yawn. All
your bright-siding friends
will not be able
to sweeten your fall.

As more workmen come
and samples are sent
for analysis it bides
its time. *I can
sit it out,* it says,
*I will teach you
how to fall.*

Anne Irwin

LIVING IN AN IDEAL WORLD

I see Brigid from number eighty approach,
listen as she describes the hole in the P&T cover
outside her house. She hands me her mobile,
I hear "rust" and "danger" as I look at a photo
of the cavity the size of her black boot.
"I'll text the other co-chairs."

We arrange a viewing, to be followed by coffee
served with gluten-free banana pancakes
topped with natural yogurt and blueberries,
and pears baked in last year's sloe gin.
*Maybe a little laudanum and smelling salts
in case the ordeal is too stressful,* I suggest.

We examine the chasm, test the surrounding area
with our toes, feel it wobble under foot.
Inclusivity and equality our motto, we email the Corpo,
Liz mentions *liability, Health and Safety,*
I propose *urgent, needs to be fixed today,*
while Mary writes adding *serious risk to our residents.*

Just as we finish our repast the van passes the window.
We drop our cups and rush to explain the catastrophic potential
of wheel-chairs, buggies, children, midnight revellers,
walking sticks, star gazers, students and joggers on iPhones
stuck in the crater designed to house telephone cables
not the population of Rockfield.

The assessor listens.
Three hours later a message from Brigid.
The manhole cover has been replaced.
          Thank you.

Peter Adair

BONFIRE

         Caught between a bonfire and a house
McClure dragged him out.
             He didn't like his looks.
The boys staked him,
     tightened the rope,
stuffed his screams with sticky tape.

        Thirty metres above him
the pallets winked at the starry sky.

When black-masked Murray
     set the flaming brand
           to the kindling,

a thousand phones clicked
          and posted to Facebook.

At this point the crowd clapped. It was observed that many spoke in tongues:
Irish, Ulster-Scots, Aramaic, Greek. Then all fell silent when the flames licked
his feet.

Next morning,
near the rain-doused embers,
a wee lad said:

"I seen him melt, ma."

Martin Malone

'FROM ONE BLUE WORLD INTO ANOTHER WORLD OF BLUE'

Stephen Sexton, *If All The World And Love Were Young* (Penguin Books, 2019), £9.99.
Sophie Collins, *Who Is Mary Sue?* (Faber and Faber, 2018), £10.99.

Two debuts from young poets of some repute, these collections come into the world 'trailing clouds of glory' and do not disappoint. In quite different ways, both seek to extend the license for what might illuminate contemporary poetry, stretching registers and form to create something both playful and profound. The apparent poetics adopted by each are also worthy of note, sharing an intertextual brio that leavens the seriousness and downright sadness of some of these poems. Where these books differ is, perhaps, in the lyric scale of each project: Sexton's debut is a moving elegiac sequence obliquely charting the loss of his mother by way of the shared signifiers of his childhood – namely those of early generation video games – whereas Collins's collection is an altogether more *heteroglossic* attempt to enact public discourse on the reception of female creativity. If this sounds a bit furrowed of brow, please don't be put off, the journey is much more entertaining than this might suggest.

That 'Penguin' imprimatur somehow seems to demand the word 'classic' as its companion. So, quite apart from the build-up of a Forward Prize win, National Poetry Competition success, and many glowing endorsements, Stephen Sexton's debut had much to live up to. I'm always delighted when work matches expectations and was delighted here. This is such a singular debut and so assured that, in places, it feels like his poetry has somewhere hit upon the profound trick of itself to produce a sequence redolent with that alchemical, world-building magic which poetry can perform. But let's take things more slowly. The collection is posited around two 'parts' that are, themselves, broken-down into a num-ber of chapters sub-divided, in turn, into short and skittish sequences, the whole deriving a sense of structural energy co-opted from computer gaming. Specifically, we are in the 16-bit world of Super Nintendo, the levels of which are used as titles throughout. I had to look all this up by the way, but, even to a digital immigrant, what's apparent here is a deeply poetic habit of mind and a collection brave enough to attempt new things with the poetic vernacular. Everywhere, there is an almost Shakespearian ambition of scope that seeks to extend the language of poetry in order to meet the modern world in new ways. This involves Sexton using the newer registers of gaming to *re-open* traditional poetic ground, or as he might put it: 'the cryptolect of ICU's / whose automatic song desires no singer's articulation' ('Donut Secret 2'). Articulate he does, though, in remarkable self-song. Herein, lies the collection's greatest achievement because, if one gets beyond the self-conscious use of Nintendolect, this is work shot-through with a hefted poetic sensibility and with tropes familiar to poetry readers everywhere. 'Lemmy's Castle' might serve as an example:

> In blue scrubs the Merlins apply various elixirs potions
> panaceas to her body some hemostatic medicines
> and a soupçon of opiate. The hospital's huge boiler plant
> rumbles hums like a volcano the wards sweltering greenhouses
> where all the patients start to look the same they are gradually
> replaced cell by corrupted cell.

This poem has been written many times, but never like this: we are on a cancer ward where the poet's mother is dying. This is a not uncommon poetic scenario, but what is most winning about the dynamic of Sexton's poetry is that, by over-layering it with the argot of his childhood video gaming and fusing that with a keen eye for the contemporary, he manages to create it anew, both for the reader and the purposes of his own grieving. It's impossible to do full justice to this technique in such a short space but I shall try to convey something of it. *Yoshi's Island, Donut Plains, Vanilla Dome, Forest of Illusions*: such phrases may be familiar to gamers of a certain demographic with whom they will find immediate resonance (they do, I asked a few younger colleagues), but to the uninitiated they carry an altogether different power as a result of Sexton's recognition of poetry innate to the language of gaming. Using this, he manages to re-offer the elegiac lyric in distinctive new voicings. Poems like 'Valley of Bowser 2' illustrate what I mean:

> On through the valley of shadow shifting strata mazes of dirt
> walls closing like mine collapses or morphine's tightness in the chest
> its heaviness and its terror.

This is such a clever and harmonious fusing of game-world scenarios with the actuality of what is happening to the poet in real life, and yet the overall *timbre* of the language deployed manages to retain a certain romanticism familiar to poetry readers. As the book progresses this becomes ever more apparent, with the gaming imagery intricately deployed to bear the weight of an age-old narrative of grief. 'Tubular' is, perhaps, an example of much of what I've tried to elucidate here, describing, as it does, the poet missing the moment of his mother's death:

> The roughed-off ends of pipes comprise a windless skyline citadel
> as though they're waiting for music if someone had the breath for it

and anyway doesn't the wind distribute breath around the world
the wind never again striking her shoulders for those final breaths
I wasn't there we had driven to McDonald's of all places ...

If All the World and Love Were Young so brilliantly manages the trick of
being familiar yet distinctive that, if Sexton is, indeed, Ireland's 'Next
Great Poet' [©RTÉ], it will be fascinating to see what he does next.

Sophie Collins' debut, *Who Is Mary Sue?*, reminds me of no-one so
much as David Jones in the bold and freewheeling spirit of poetic inven-
tiveness on display. Like many a good book, this also has the virtue of
facing down reader expectation; indeed, it makes a point of doing so in its
apparent purpose of teaching us something about heavily gendered
presumption when it comes to the reception of female writing. *Is this
poetry?* is always a good question for the author of a poetry collection to
have their reader ask, since it admits the possibility of extending our sense
of what is viable and new in the form. And here, what might reasonably
be described as 'feminist verse-essay' is executed with such panache that
its import is rendered all-the-more effective by it being such fun to read.
Yes, *fun*. This is not to underplay the seriousness of the issues taken up by
Collins, but her greatest achievement here is to platform the playfulness
of the book's poetics and take the reader along with her.

Essentially, the collection is a performative reading of fan fiction,
Mary Sue being, as the jacket blurb has it, 'an idealised and implausibly
flawless character: a female archetype that can infuriate audiences for its
perceived narcissism'. However, these perceptions are archly reflexive,
shedding as much light upon the received assumptions made about
female writing in general. The book also speaks to the forever-delayed
nature of professional progress for millennials, specifically (though not
exclusively) in the arts. If all this sounds a bit 'meta' it is, but entertainingly
so. Collins uses an intertextual approach to draw upon a peppy range
of references that obliquely reveal her purpose: everything from authorial address, dialogue, exposition, academic-style prose, anecdote, flash-
fiction, quotes from real-life women writers like Sharon Olds and Rachel
Cusk, and fictive or real journal notes. The overall effect is personae-rich,
palimpsestic, and dramatic, with each component contributing to a lively
dialogue among themselves. This is expertly sequenced and handled with
a light touch, quite difficult to convey here but typified in the following
selection, each of which, bar one, constitutes a single 'poem':

> 'I don't know if I should be sending this to you,' wrote one young
> author in her cover letter to a magazine. 'I'm afraid it's a Mary Sue.
> Only I don't know what that is.'

Thus Mary Sue becomes, in my eyes, an unwitting embodiment of
the double standard of content.

I note that, in literary fiction, when a female writer's female
protagonist *is* considered up to scratch, she is often taken to be a
thinly disguised version of the author's *non*-idealised self.

and:

I begin to collect quotations, responses.

While didactic intent can occasionally skim over common experience (the
solely gendered conflation of authored persona with authorial self is a
moot point), the manner in which Collins executes her argument makes
for a right rollicking read. Her points are important and embrace a far
broader range of female experience than I may have given the impression
of here. There are, also, some truly memorable lines of poetry: 'The future is an eye that I don't dare look into' ('Dear No. 24601'), for instance,
or the hint of trafficked voices in 'Beauty Milk':

I don't matter.
I am a blemish,
a fragment,
an apartment.

I am a multiplication
and a made-up belief.
I am nothing for days afterwards.

That the book engenders its own woozy sense of allegorical self-revela-
tion along the way – a sort of contemporary feminist *Piers Plowman* – is
also much to its credit. And, as I say, while demanding serious engagement with its rhetorical purpose, *Who Is Mary Sue?* makes for a hugely
entertaining read. Well worth checking out.

Kelly Creighton

PERCEPTION OF DEPTH *OR* DEEP END

When I came home from Ayr I let it ferment.
Curious how you can know a thing and try to deny it to yourself.
You took your time walking down steps, unsure
a poor perception of depth,
the phrase sprung from my old career working with adults
who lived with difficulties learning.

You flapped on holidays and all that list
but no   she almost grasped the potty a few months ago
or maybe it was a mischance,
she said a strip of words in the park she didn't say again,
that line from a song she echoed ...
but she doesn't look me in the eye when I call her name,
yet she does at other times, intently and intensely.
She is the most affectionate child at Jo Jingles,
not joining, okay, but looking at her reflection,
running into my arms and lots of kisses.

That night, your father went to bed, and I opened
the laptop and Googled: signs of autism
disrupted sleep and upset
screaming or giggling
Yes, both. But giggling?
that was it   the point at which your life
cannot return back to how it was.
I read on in tears, going and waking your father
to confirm it   I had just broken my own heart.
I'd phone the doctor the next day
to see what could be done about that.

Brian Kirk

GOOGLING MY PARENTS

When I Googled my parents there were no matching results, only
traces of others who bore the same names, living counterfeit lives

that failed to reflect the authenticity of monochrome days I recall
in that house by the railway line, where the sun shone all summer,

where huge ash trees waved their hysterical arms in March winds,
and a thin frost painted a dull world silver on the shortest days.

My parents don't exist in the world, real or virtual, but are trapped
in stacks of wrinkled snaps; they look out at me with unseeing eyes,

perplexed, uncertain, frozen in a moment snatched from time. I know
there's no option to reboot, no going back except through memory's

patched-up matinee. From time to time, to kick-start reminiscence,
I read their names in stone among a host of other names on stones

ranged on a blanket of land that rolls down to the sea near home.
Perhaps the mind is a hard drive scanning the residue of lives

no longer with us, its circuits switching on and off, firing in dreams
where the dead arise, their voices talking out of the bright cloud.

Bebe Ashley

from THERE IS A REASON THIS IS CALLED SHAME

in a different universe the boys met at the bus stop
avoiding eye-contact with a pile of strawberry milk sick
the bus was too far away to be a comfortable wait
so the boy who transferred schools mid-year invited
the boy who he had never spoken to before home
then fought electrons of nervous energy when he said yes

when the needle dropped slowly onto the vinyl
heavy beats of dubstep pulsed from the record player
the boy who didn't know vinyl could sound that way
threw his head forward and crashed the tip of his teeth
against the green glass of his beer bottle to laugh

later when the conversation got a little personal
the boy who hid secrets sat easily at the electric piano
and played so tenderly that the room felt different
and it was possible things had changed between them

★★★

the boy who lived a thousand lives in a single day
said something careless and everything stopped

silence   stretched   between   them

the boy who thinks they should take things slower
cannot return any text messages and evades sleep

affinity   brings   them   back   together

Alison Brackenbury

7 AUGUST, 1983

Raw, starless midnight. On the way
before my only child was born
we reached your parents' house. I stayed,
lower back seized, quick waters gone.
You hurried from me through the dark.
You heaved the saddle in your hands
which they must drive to stables, back
for lessons, on arena's sands.

I knew that parents, friends could snap
all our worst futures would career
from that torn night, that shuddered stop
through pains. Next, I glimpsed, ten days late,
by lanes, parked pram, my horse's ears.
New-born, I scaled the padlocked gate.

Dane Holt

FORD ESCORT

Through sheer force of will she got me into school
for my final final-year exam – GCSE Eng Lit. (haha!) –
despite my muffled protests and my quick-thinking
with the flannel, soaked in (not too warm!) warm water
to complement my clutching, guttural complaints;

and despite the white Ford Escort – O, childhood! –
that brought to mind my Dad, who, she said,
would have to "aspire to be *this* useless,"
and had "at least worked once!"
Did it leave the factory and then the forecourt

rust-speckled, like the last recorded egg
of some dim, flightless bird; was it geared
solely towards missing mornings and (logically thereafter)
whole days of school, and warning after final warning
from work? Either way, I'm revising on the fly as she's holding it together

round roundabouts, through (uh hum)
amber traffic lights – *Mum! Muuum! Identify the metaphor
in this poem* – and between the school gates, barely slowing down
before shooing me, protesting still, out the door
behind the driver's seat – the only one that'll open.

Eimear Bourke

FRANKIE BLACK

Sundays 11 a.m.
the whole Northside of town
would congregate in St. Oliver Plunkett's church.

The far side of the Boyne
comfortable Southsiders,
or those looking for a lie-in,
would convoke in St. Mary's at 1 p.m.

I'm not sure how it works now,
now that mass is dead.

Where people get their news.
Or feel their shame.

Richard Hayes

WHEREOF ONE CANNOT SPEAK

John W Sexton, *Futures Pass* (Salmon Poetry, 2018), €12.
Rachael Hegarty, *May Day 1974* (Salmon Poetry, 2019), €14.
Anne Fitzgerald, *Vacant Possession* (Salmon Poetry, 2017), €12.

By and large we receive poems one by one, the 'collection' being precisely
that, a gathering together into book form of various individual pieces of
work, sometimes loosely, sometimes firmly bound into a kind of shape,
but within which the individual poem breathes and has its own life and,
indeed, out of which it can be extracted to exist quite happily alone. It
is interesting therefore to come across three collections so insistent on
being received as books, that is, dependent for their effect on the inter-
play between various component parts and the larger whole, reliant on
the reader's willingness to stay with the scheme of the thing across one
hundred or more pages and scores of poems and, as it were, to suppress
the experience of the individual poem in favour of an appreciation of
the overall volume. The three collections here, each in its own way, give
primacy to something beyond the individual (invariably lyric) poem; their
ambition resides in their reaching for effects that cannot be achieved one
poem at a time, an ambition that is highly commendable.

Sexton's imposes the loosest structure, depends least on overall design
for its effects. In this case, the book is an exercise in impersonation in the
manner of Pessoa – or, perhaps more accurately, Sexton's is an exercise
in ventriloquism – and impresses for the daring of the concept and the
consistency with which it is executed. Sexton explains in a foreword the
nature of the experiment: enduring a period of writer's block in 2008, he
created a poet who could write while he could not, a figure called Jack
Brae Curtingstall. Curtingstall found a means of expression in the
blogosphere – Facebook and other forums being vast empty walls on
which the poems could be scratched as a kind of electronic graffiti. The
notion that the poem once it appeared was deemed published – meaning
it could not appear elsewhere – gave a certain freedom to the enterprise,
a liberating hopelessness, according to Sexton. And so, what we have in
Futures Pass are the jottings and musings of this Jack Brae Curtingstall,
excursions given permanence here while understanding themselves to
have a kind of impermanence – poems strangely sure of themselves,
convinced though they are of their own ephemerality.

Inevitably, this manifests itself in a number of meta-poems, such as 'A
Uriel Lands Waste in My Head', a reinvention of 'The Waste Land':

Our April had the coolest moths, breeding
maggots out of the dead nap, fixing
emery eggs higher on the curtaining ...

'How the Ninety Hidden Anarchist Saints Travelled Through Time on a Diet of Worms' might be the title of a modern art masterpiece (I'm reminded of the titles of the artist Robert Williams's works), and is a curious excursion into the nature of writing, in which Martin Luther's ninety-five theses are 'ninety- / five verses of revolution, paper / cog in an abstract self-winding mantle- / / clock', as good a description of *Futures Pass* as any. Throughout the book, the poems draw attention to themselves, whether by formal means – there are a number of formally very successful poems, including a villanelle ('So Softly Into Light') and, rarity of rarities, a sestina ('Somewhere in the Pig') – or through variations on punctuation (Sexton deploys a wide range of keyboard characters to function as pauses and breaks in the lines, including '<', '/', '\', and '{'). But this is not a book of tricks and gimmicks; nor is it a book for post-structuralist literary critics only to salivate over. This is a book of many pleasures for every reader; after all, as we are told,

Poetry is the squashed frogs two summers ago
all over the road with their spawn blown out

Poetry can be many things but is most likely
and most certainly not the thing you say it is

In the end, whether this is the voice of Sexton or some other is entirely irrelevant: the impersonation has freed up a space that has been delightfully and energetically filled with funny, fantastic, and life- and poetry-affirming poems.

Much more structured – indeed, highly schematised – is Rachael Hegarty's remarkable *May Day 1974*. The book establishes a simple format. It has, broadly, thirty-three sections, one each for every one of the 33 dead from the Dublin and Monaghan bombings of 17 May 1974, bombings the author herself survived. Each victim is first recalled by name, his or her age is given, and then a short, factual description ('Married, housewife, and living in Portmarnock', and so on). Secondly, in the form of what the author calls a 'docu-sonnet', we are given an excerpt from the witness statements from the inquiry into the individual's death. The author's foreword confirms that the sonnets are 'crafted verbatim'; where the craft is in these testimonies, the manipulation, is hard to tell: each reads complete, as if the family member spoke in fourteen line bursts. 'I am James Croarkin, brother of the deceased, Thomas Croarkin', begins one of these sonnets, and ends 'Och, my mother lived, but she never really got over that, you know.' The author suggests that 'allowances for metre' were important in crafting the sonnets; this is not immediately audible, but this 'found' poetry is no less powerful for that: indeed, it is more powerful for carrying with it the authentic rawness of the emotions of the bereaved. The evidence of Paddy Doyle into the death of the O'Brien family (John, 24; Anna, 22; Jacqueline, 17 months; Anne-Marie, 5 months) – 'They're after killing a hell of a lot of people. / I don't think I'm really the same after that. / It was the sight, the scenery in the morgue, / I think that knocked a bit out of me, you know'– lives long after the book has been read.

Each section finishes with an original poem that gives a voice to the dead person. In many cases these poems celebrate life, the simple pleasures of work, whether in a garden or in an office, beginning romances or the delights of a marriage. Threatening, intruding on this day-to-day innocence, come undefined 'strangers'. 'But the stranger / who sits facing the door, / his eyes shifting / all over the place – // watch him, / watch him like a hawk', warns Archie Harper in his poem – he was a victim of the Monaghan bombing. 'Them strangers make me want / to race back home / to hug, feel the bones of me husband', says Peggy White, also a victim. Most telling here, most moving, are the pages that represent the dead children – Baby O'Neill, child of Dublin victim Edward John O'Neill (aged 39), stillborn three months after its father's death; and Baby Doherty, who was never born as her mother, Colette Doherty (21), was still carrying her when she was killed in Dublin – pages where, though the name is given, there is no voice to accompany the name. The individual lyric, in other words, is reduced to nothing; the power of the book is here entirely dependent on its form. The book seeks a language for remembrance and finds it not in any of the well-constructed lyric poems, nor in the deliberation of the docu-sonnets, nor in the litany of names, but in the blank spaces between.

In some ways similar to *May Day 1974*, Anne Fitzgerald's stunning *Vacant Possession* is also a personal history. The most immediately intriguing part of the book is a single photograph that appears late on. The picture is of the Georgian interior of Temple Hill House, a place run by the Sisters of Charity from which many hundreds of children were sent for adoption to America from the 1930s onwards. In the photograph, which is of a door opening to an empty room, the cold tiled floor speaks to institutional convenience, the emptiness of the picture to institutional indifference, and yet one cannot but be struck by the serenity of the place – the design is, in eighteenth-century style, immaculately balanced and, in its own, still way, beautiful. This captures well, I think, the aesthetic of *Vacant Possession* which, though it is an incredibly angry book, is a book that, in its careful uncovering of the author's past, is poised, deliberate and studied.

Aidan Mathews, in a very interesting introduction, sees the book as composed of 'three trimesters of lyric poetry'. The first of these, the first section of the book, is a series of love poems, poems exploring in Matthews' understanding 'the body of the self'. These poems create some ambivalence around the addressee. 'I stumble under the weight / of your magnetic field', we read in 'Compass'; who the 'you' might be here, that vagueness, is territory that the collection itself will explore.

The bulk of the book concerns itself with the archaeology of the author's own past ('You' as her infant self?) and her mother's past ('You' as her lost mother?), as they moved through St Patrick's Infant Hospital and Nursery College, as it was called. The electric charge in the book comes from the current running between the second and the third trimester of poetry in Mathews' formulation: 'the body of the single and the singular mother, both natural and adoptive' meeting head on 'the body of the state, those political interlopers we call circumstance and history and the way things are (or were)'. The book leads towards 'Finding Myself in Werburgh Street', where the author reads her name in a ledger:

> Not five minutes shy of two hours I lean into
> a past of myself, as unrecognisable as a wild
>
> pearl, iridescent and luminous as the shell itself
> or my fingerprint smudged. Reading my birth
>
> name given is like a foreign language forged
> in copperplate, a kind of twisted mother-tongue
>
> as if finding the needle, without eye or haystack,
> purposefully sent to hit a dead end by the grace
>
> and blessings of the Archbishop's handmaidens.

There follows, a number of poems later, 'Finding You at Fifty', a photo-graph of 'you', that is, the author's mother:

> Something in a trick of light betrays
> our line of beauty, different but the same.
>
> What with a similar left shock of white hair
> I know I am of you. See my own reflection
>
> look back at me for near the first time,
> sure in the knowledge of what's in a name.

From the depths of emotion evoked in the poems in the first section and the rage towards the State and its institutions in the postscript, is forged, in *Vacant Possession*, a series of subtle tender, fearful, frustrated investigations of the meaning of daughterhood and motherhood, of family, of personal identity, and ultimately of what it means to love. This helps explain the enigmatic photograph: it is a picture of an institution, for sure, and an attempt to capture a certain terror in the stony silence; but the serenity of the photograph is of the peace that comes from forgetting, I think. The author includes the photograph as a demonstration of the temptation to aestheticise trauma, the temptation to settle for a kind of crafted peace. The book tells against itself in this respect for the author refuses to accept peaceful resolution — 'a trinity of control and culpability pervades', she writes in the postscript (note the use of the present tense), 'within the Catholic Church, the Irish Free State and its Religious Institutions specifically established to contain, to profit from and to manage the lives of those who bore children outside marriage and the little lives born outside of the bands of holy matrimony.' It is this refusal to resolve that is what is most extraordinary about this piercing, intelligent book.

Seán Kelly

JULY

Awake early, the room already bright,
the necklace you left behind still on the locker.
I should have dumped it by now.

I knew it was over when you started smoking again –
arms folded at the back door, staring across the lawn.

Yesterday you instagrammed from Florence,
your hair blonde now, wearing my Willie Nelson t-shirt,
blowing a kiss at the statue of David.

We were in Greece this time last year,
hiking around Aegina's stone and weed mountains.
You kept stopping while I caught up.

We kissed at the top, took selfies, shared a can of warm beer
then photographed what remained of the temple of Adonis –
a headless statue made of ash and clay
with a wasps' nest in the dark of its hollow chest.

Zosia Kuczyńska

CLIFFHANGER
        – *after Robert Banks Stewart*

The third time a question is asked of us
you break the silence and answer

and when I think you're not going to wish me good morning
you wish me good morning

and when the driver stops the car
you ask them why we've stopped

and when the wrong thing is being recycled
you are there to prevent it

and in the jaws of a guided tour
you ask when it'll be over

and listening to terrible music
you say the music's terrible

and getting locked out whilst moving plants
you try the other door

and finding a way to leave the house
you don't leave me behind.

Geraldine Mitchell

BULLY BOY

While other children
screamed and raced
around the garden

he worried
who would pick him
when the games began inside

follow my leader
stick a tail on the donkey
musical chairs

braced for rejection
he'd volunteer
to have a scarf

tied tightly round
his eyes
for *blind man's buff*

then stand
the centre of the rumpus
as noises fell away

and he explored
the inside of his head
where everything went quiet

like when he slid his whole face
underwater
in the bath

he felt a power well up
then breached the silence
suddenly

dealt out
rough justice
on the scattering room

Angela McCabe

A DAY'S WORK

Slow walking to a pattern, the figure of 8,
a mathematical symbol of infinity.

Wood, coal, feathers,
black tails, matches.

Descending the mezzanine of the art college
something in me snapped when I saw him.

Chicken wire for boundaries, obstacles,
fences, barriers, Belfast security gates, 'no go' areas.

Scrim over his head, awakening links
with the darkness that surrounded us.

Soldiers everywhere in the city on patrol
with machine guns, Saracens reading:

Report: Confidential telephone
Freephone 0800 666 999.

Twice a day we passed through huts in the city centre,
uniformed people, body searches.

I thought of Moscow, walking along main streets
brown, grey, khaki uniforms, threatening hats.

To wander into side streets
or park to admire wild flowers,

out of pale blue air they'd come, point guns.

I remembered the expressions on faces
in Smolensk,the same look on people's in Belfast.

This Performance Artist silently communicates:

'Freedom of imagination and play has been
replaced by dark control.'

I worked with paint, smeared it over my body
rolled in sand and peat moss,

cycled the streets of Belfast
balloons tied to my arms holding me up.

Helen Pizzey

CONDOLENCE

Months have come and gone like doctors,
each with its succession of head-shaking sorrow.

I want no more petalled apologies,
no more thorns of shock or surprise.
Let my comfort be immutably ugly;
black, not subject to beautiful decay.

The wilted, dusty tongues of flowers
seek one salt tear to satisfy;
scant vapour of one dry sigh
is all they will receive.

Mine is a withered house.
There is no water here.

Grace Wells

THE RULE OF THREE

Susan Millar DuMars, *Naked: New and Selected Poems* (Salmon Poetry, 2019), €14.
Eileen Sheehan, *The Narrow Way of Souls* (Salmon Poetry, 2018), €12.
Kate Newmann, *Ask Me Next Saturday* (Summer Palace Press, 2018), £10/€10.

Here are three poets who in three different ways are saying, *World, you can do better than this. Mankind, you can do better than this.*

Susan Millar DuMars' 2008 debut collection *Big Pink Umbrella* sparkled with electric candour. It fizzed energy. Time has not dated or dimmed those earlier poems; they shine out of her *Naked: New and Selected Poems* with the same breezy effortlessness that first marked Millar DuMars as a poet to watch. But now they stand as a testament to the ways the poet's voice has subtly altered over her prolific decade of publication. Perhaps under the pressure of what she refers to in a recent poem – 'Horatio, After' – as 'The quiet compromises / of growing up', something of her youthful, piquant zest has slowly surrendered to a mature and measured authority.

'And I look again and am different, / different even from the woman / who boarded the plane. Somehow smaller. / Older', Millar DuMars admits in 'On Arrival', but what each of her poetry collections suggests is not a diminishment in voice, but rather an intensification of potency, a honing of strengths that were evident all along. In 'Don't Try To Be Good' she asserts 'misfortune cures you / like smoke / makes that meaty heart of yours / taste saltier', conjuring a sense of the briny resistance she has repeatedly thrown into the face of injustice, oppression, and censorship of the female.

Naked is the perfect title for this compilation from a poet whose work is centred in the courage to tell the truth about the world, and to bare her many-sided selves. DuMars has never sought to shock, never disrobed for the sake of it, but rather gyred her focus to a central enquiry of how stark feminine realities may best be expressed through subtle poetics. She's simultaneously refreshingly full-frontal, while maintaining dignity, composure and control.

Reading these selections side by side gives voice to many different types of nakedness. In 'Braid', there's the raw vulnerability of girlhood. In 'Ash', the bare truth of romantic relationship gone awry. There seems to be no territory that Millar DuMars won't scrutinise or expose; we're not refused entry to her dream-world, her bedroom, or her body, which she uproariously celebrates in 'let the dog' – and poignantly reflects on in her recent 'Dirty Word':

And we can't talk about
what goes in or out of it
and I have to petition
just to gain control of it
and you wonder why
I'm of two minds about it?

My sweetest place. The cruelest taunt.
I try to write its name down. Can't.

The selection of poems taken from *The God Thing* (2013) elegantly expands
her enquiry towards the spiritual. The poems track the ineffable's elusive
spoor as she navigates the vagaries of life, and the loss and death of loved
ones. In 'Undiscovered', she stands humbly before that mystery:

I remember her body
just after – shrunk,
the skin a new skin,
cold and slack as a white sail
on a windless day.
Something had gone. Though we can't
see the breeze, we know when
it stops blowing. Something had gone.
I only want to know what it was.

Throughout *Naked: New and Selected Poems*, the intimate, personal voyage
is interspersed with poems that consider the raw world. 'Mud' succeeds
in condensing the shifting responsibilities of modern warfare to a single
page. 'Reverse' rewinds the terrible moments of JFK's assassination to
lay that tragedy bare. Whatever darkness Millar DuMars' eye falls on, she
portrays the scene with an exactness of detail and a gild of light – a grace
– that enables the reader to keep looking and not turn away. In 'Pumpkin
Song', the pumpkin speaks for the poet: 'Carve for me a mouth / and I
will sing away the darkness; / put a tune to truth.'
    Millar DuMars' own particular song, the leitmotif that returns in all
her collections, is a delight in ordinary things; the way the humdrum can
be a salve against all harm. A cat, a cappuccino, a tea-stained mug, socks
worn in bed, the hanging of laundry, or the discussion of a sonnet over
breakfast, are all cornerstones. As she sweetly confesses in 'Nothing in
This life',

I'm crying
in the middle of Shop Street
because all of this
will go. This gorgeous confusion.

The song will end.
The street will empty.
Nothing in this life is as hard
as leaving it.

The final line of the book, the final line of the poem 'Don't Tell the Witch',
simply states: 'No spell stronger than this loved life'. It's a line that
encapsulates the potency of Millar DuMars' decade of work: four strong
collections from a wise, witty, and deeply romantic poet in love with life,
the feminine, her body, her home and husband. A poet who has continuously married the naked power of her voice with indomitable language in
defence of a cherished world.

Eileen Sheehan opens her new collection, *The Narrow Way of Souls*,
with three framing poems. 'A is for Alzheimer, C is for Carer', and 'The
Greatest' are both poignant portraits of her mother's long illness and the
poet's caring role. Then, quite suddenly, we're plunged into a parallel
Otherworld. 'The Stray' opens with the imperative:

If you must enter the fairy field at evening,
fill your pockets with iron.

The poem is a caution about walking 'forever in circles / unable to tell
the gate from the hedge, / tell the grass from the sky' – a folkloric parallel
to losing years of one's life to an illness, or caring for an ailing parent.
Soon the narrative that pertains to her mother's illness and passing
dissolves like a stream gone underground, only to re-emerge in the
closing sequence of the collection with the breath-taking prose poem
'Pre-emptive'. By the time we read it, we've gone on a mythic journey.

The morning of her funeral. I don't know the me in the
mirror. Motherless and twelve-years older than before.

Before diagnosis; before belief; before anger; before illness
proper; disease undeniable; before slow decline. Before she
began to show up dead in my dreams. Before every morning
I was surprised to see her still there ...

The piece beautifully captures the long years and narrow pathway of
soul-making that Sheehan has been engaged with. Like a magical look-
ing-glass in a fairytale, 'Pre-emptive' reflects the context in which much
of this collection must have been created – and makes it all the more
admirable. For this is a striking collection of both beguiling and elemental
poems, whose totemic images stir our earliest learnings: bird feather,
road, river, moon, bright star, girl child.

Sheehan's continuous dives in and out of folklore and the magical are much like Sive's fall into the pool where the Salmon of Knowledge swims, the poet plunging the reader between all the worlds, evoking conscious and unconscious responses. Repeatedly she puts tactile material into our hands, only to have it morph or shape-shift, so we never quite know what we're really holding. And there's a lyrical transience, a loss felt even as we apprehend what's there.

Reading the collection brought to mind Heaney's lines from 'Blackberry picking': 'You ate that first one and its flesh was sweet / Like thickened wine: summer's blood was in it'. Each of these poems is intoxicating. But the summer blood that colours them all, is assuredly the deeply engaging soul of Eileen Sheehan, part enchantress, part magician, wise crone, lost daughter, and child of the earth. Her journey through *The Narrow Way of Souls* is not so much poetry-as-spiritual-autobiography, but poetry-as-soul-making.

Perhaps soul work is always done under duress, like the completing of Psyche's labours, or by getting lost in a briar forest and falling victim to the kind of trickster Devil that Sheehan warns against in 'Advice to Suburban Daughters':

> Be aware,
> the pulse of blood
> at your throat
> is the music
> that calls him.
>
> Don't be duped
> by his genteel manners,
>
> how he charms your father,
> how he makes your brother feel awkward
> in his own skin.
>
> Call on your mother
> to stand with you at the door.
>
> Under no circumstances
> invite him in.

Often, when contemporary writers revisit folklore, returning with Oisín to modern-day streets, or re-entering a taciturn, old Grimm village, they snip at the material with sharp, post-modern scissors and fashion redundant new clothes for the emperor. But in response to our dire times,

Sheehan is deeply aware of how badly we need re-enchantment and a quickening of all that invigorates the psyche and reconnects us to life. Rarely has a poetry collection provided so many renewing and revitalising poems.

In most fairytales there are three gifts or wishes, three tasks, tests or trials, three chances to get it right and break the spell that holds the land in crisis. Like a third, youngest sister challenged with an impossible fairytale quest, Sheehan, the 'dark-haired child' ('My Father, Long Dead'), returns with the unattainable achieved. And if this were a book of thirds, which it isn't quite, it would divide into Sheehan's recent autobiographical material, the bitter realities of small-town Ireland, and her parallel folk-loric realm. Each territory informs the other, and her braiding of these three strands creates a fascinating matrix, a multi-layering of themes which is so successful that it's never quite clear what is lore, what real-life. 'Crawthumpers' takes to task Ireland's small-town 'Gossipers, clittering at every corner, / predicting the fall of so-and-so's daughter.' Does 'clittering' even exist as a real-world word? Might it be the verb of a thwarted clitoris turned to the dark arts? The poem ends with the spell-binding condemnation of the crawthumpers:

> Wielding, without understanding,
> the power of the cunt, the power of the tongue.

There is a deep, cathartic joy in reading this collection, as if all the mixed-up, muddled-up wrongs of fairytale and real-life have at last been redeemed. Here, curses are lifted, and all restrictions placed on girl children are brought to a timely end. This is unforgettable writing, a true book of winter cures. Sheehan has taken a pathless way through dark woods to tumble onto our table the contents of a magical sack. For long years to come, *The Narrow Way of Souls* will flit through the waking and sleeping mind of Irish poetry, stirring all who hear of it, like news of a white hart seen again in the land, propelling even kings to rise from their feasting, and set off after in perpetual hunt.

Kate Newmann's *Ask Me Next Saturday* is a book of repossessions – territories, histories, biographies; often inspired by familiar stories and subject-matter that we might be forgiven for thinking already done-to-death. But Newmann lifts her material as she might pick up a spent flyer from a long-gone circus, to conjure marvels more exciting than anything the big top ever showed. Her opening poem concerns the sinking of the *Titanic*, but the familiar story is created anew by unexpected images of 438 gallons of ice cream, 190 bundles of cheese, 2500 pounds of sausage, and beguiling descriptions of …

the tapestries the 8000 cigars

the 11 cases of orchids
the 40,000 eggs   oh shell break
and yolk float

seawater made
a monstrous dough
of the 250 barrels of flour

a macabre laundry
of the 45,000 napkins
and 18,000 bed sheets

But the real heart of the poem, and that which engenders the tender title
'Until the Next Time All My Love', is the lost mail, *'until the next time all /
my love I hope to hear from // you soon dear dearest sir darling dearest'*, the
'soluble sentiments' of innumerate letters dissolved into the Atlantic. It is
the contents of these lost mail-sacks in particular that Newmann reclaims,
restoring dignity to the individuals that sent them, and the expectant
minds that never received them.

The poem 'Repossessing Anne Naysmith' appears to be another
restoration of dignity. But it's hard to know how many layers of irony
Newmann has stacked into lines that chart Naysmith's loss of home, room,
and piano, the 'very ribs and air / that allowed my gift to live'. Following
her eviction, Anne Naysmith spent twenty years living in a Ford Consul
until irritated neighbours had the council tow it away. The pianist lived
then in 'bushes by the tube station', only to be killed when a passing lorry
struck her down. After a moving litany of dispossessions, the poem ends

You might as well go ahead now
and repossess my voice.

Newmann has knowingly taken possession of the pianist's voice, but the
result is a striking paean to Anne Naysmith. Though it can't rewind the
years of living rough, it gives them the decency of commemoration – a
memorialization that lives long in the reader's mind.

There's a similar sense of rehabilitation in 'Stoat's Tail, Green Butt', a
biographical portrait of reclusive Megan Boyd, who tied salmon flies for
notable patrons including Prince Charles. Boyd never fished herself, but
'knew / each loch and river, each spate / and stretch and current'. The
poem catches something of Megan Boyd's eccentricities, but in so doing,
charts the shy beauties within her peculiar life. The poem also gives
Newmann the chance to deeply inhabit the life of the salmon, to

repossess the clean waters and freedoms so many have already lost:

> They don't feed in fresh water, the salmon, so the fly
> was a call to something unthought, some needed, unheeded
> like a soul desire – some instinct between colour and pulse
> like poetry, or a last taunting chance at the past.

Kate Newmann's writing has a particular clarity to it, a pellucidity of clean words. But it contains something more, a presence which won't be described with an adjective. In the clear pool of her well, minute bubbles trickle upwards, provoking questions – invisible presences that call you back again and again in attempt to demystify the enigma of what she's doing. What is this other thing that she infuses into plain speech?

These transpicuous presences are most often her poetic gifts, but they are also sometimes the fascinating research details that Newmann has filigreed into poetic form. She does this particularly effectively in 'Ataturk', a luminous portrait of the last days of the controversial 'father' of modern Turkey, which ends in lines that could have been written by Hafiz or Rumi:

> *This time*
> *Alone*
> *One body with one soul*
> *He was a garden*
> *With plants and birdsong*
> *Moving through him like rain*

The poem is typical of the remarkable way *Ask Me Next Saturday* continuously re-enters familiar histories so that they may be told anew. This is a striking book of narratives, a 'wingspan of sorrow wider than us' ('The Wounded Heron') arcing over poems of loss, pulling us back into the lives and small heroics of the forgotten. Like Shakespeare's Ariel, who rode the winds for Prospero, Newmann's subject-matter has her dive to the bottom of the Atlantic, journey through the jungles of Sumatra, enter into forbidden territories such as Mount Athos in Greece, and look long at women in display-cases in Amsterdam – all for the purpose of repossession. *Ask Me Next Saturday* is ultimately a very female book, and contributes, like Susan Millar DuMars and Eileen Sheehan, to a remaking of the feminine, a restoration of the parts of ourselves that were long ago scattered across time and place.

Tim Dwyer

UNCERTAIN SALVATION

Far enough into spring,
back road to the women's prison
canopied with growing leaves.
Last night's wind and rain
has dusted the surface
with golden maple blossoms.

My last day of work
behind these double steel fences
and grey razor wire.
I hear a mocking bird's reveille
in the cedar beyond the compound,

and I see my mother.
Imagined catastrophes hide
her real tragedies –
how long to brew the tea,
whether to sleep
with the window slightly ajar.

On this date she arrived in New York,
truly believing the sidewalks
would be paved with gold.

Once she told me a redemption story.
We have two lives:
one we learn from,
one we live.

I have been sentenced
to my second life.

Note: the italicised lines are a paraphrase from the film,
The Natural.

Jamie Stedmond

NOTES ON A HOLIDAY (FRAGMENTS)

The radiators were going cold.
A CCTV camera faced away from the hotel
on a tall pole,
watching always the people I watched sometimes.

We agree that if you fall in the river that you will die;
and isn't it odd, to have death built into a town,
happily running underneath us on giant grey legs.

You were overcome at two points: once by heights,
and the second time, by your aversion to shell-fish.

Two grey flies against grey sky
          steady walked
          along Memtwerge
headed to the Abbey on Mutton Island.

The seagulls: the jocks of the docks,
the crows: goths

Eyre Square
  laid-out geometrically
    crossed haphazardly
       in the rain

A holiday is a hollow-shell of glass,
which cracks, as the train tracks
rewind

– I used to really enjoy my life
before I knew that I was living it.

B. Anne Adriaens

CONSIDER THE CARETAKER

The caretaker must be an old man,
confined to the downstairs room
of someone else's derelict dream.
His lit window stares down at you
through the smooth beech trunks
as the 38 bus rumbles past
the steep wooded slope that cradles
and lifts the turreted silhouette.

After the light is turned off,
the power no longer supplied,
after he surrendered
to dry rot's weeping serpents
and their multitude of spores,
you trespass upon the territory
that was his charge and find
a rusty screwdriver,
an empty canister of sealant,
a waxed tablecloth. Just enough
to allow you to slip under his skin,
ageing frame rattling inside a brick cage,
skirting the walls of those upper rooms
where the floor sank to the basement.
He peers at the first stars
through tiers of jagged joists and rafters.
He sits on the stairs and reads
from a soil-scented book, by the green glow
of the ivy-covered window.

The rubble on the ground floor rises,
fuses back into a solid structure
facing the grate where he lights a fire.
You leave him to this peace
you could never have,
walk out from under the shadow,
damp and cold an afterthought
smashing into your bones.
You cast one more glance
through a Pentax lens,
don't press the shutter release
but turn your back
on a place you would've called home.

Eoin Hegarty

SEA LIFE, BRAY

A low-flow presence,
cymbal chime or tuning fork

humming to itself, tingling through
the darkened rooms. A tortoise

on a stone – slow foot
and ancient head panning left

and right over a pool of slippery
light. Tidelines touch and go

in a fringe across the pane. Gills,
fins, slippery presences. A stingray

sweeps past, shoulder high
like a great bird. *Moon jellyfish*

ghost alone, threads pulsing
in the blue dark. And sharks

circle, endlessly, their display-case
setting – their restless searching

within the box – our breath
and hands clouding the glass.

Thomas McCarthy

THE PRICE OF EVERYTHING

Edited by Benjamin Keatinge, *Making Integral: Critical Essays on Richard Murphy* (Cork University Press, 2019), €39 hb.

Richard Murphy's poetry and his long career reminds us that every poet is, ultimately, *sui generis*. It is the object of criticism to beg to differ, to find connections and proofs of influence in the work, in the letters and in the life. Murphy, who was born in 1927 and died last year, took a life in poetry upon himself as any other great Anglo-Irish gentleman might have taken on a new project in estate management or house-building. The Ormsby blood in him, like the Pollexfen blood in Yeats, meant that we would end up with a great edifice rather than a profligate embarrassment. If you compare his career with that of another literary Anglo-Irishman, Arland Ussher of Co Waterford, you'll see what I mean by the word 'edifice'. Ussher's chaotic and peripatetic artistic life tells us about the varieties of personality available within the tight Anglo-Irish world. Murphy, unlike Ussher, would never have married a family housekeeper: we know from the sheer quality of Murphy's verse-craft that he would always choose society above comfort. The severity and beauty of his poetry is a unique event in post-War Irish writing; and the severity of his beauty, both personal and poetic, was an exotic presence in an otherwise fairly homogenous bog-trotting Irish poetry world.

Benjamin Keatinge has done brilliant work with this new critical work, *Making Integral*. These essays by some of the best surveyors in the field, try to integrate materials that are ultimately irreconcilable: Irish Protestant memory and Irish national destiny. The two can never be fully integrated because the one has always yearned for the other's failure – the Boyne victory for one meant the defeat of the other, the creation of grand estates meant the humiliation and dispossession of millions. Possession and loss, inheritance and Planter self-delusion, history and its fabrications, public glory and narcissism, sexual frustration and social identity, all play their role in the drama of Richard Murphy's life; a life that is preserved for us forever in *The Pleasure Ground; Poems 1952-2012* and the quirky and bold memoir, *The Kick*. Murphy was always very honest with himself; he knew when he held deluded historical positions. Both *The Battle of Aughrim* and *The God Who Eats Corn* are complex and thrilling attempts by the poet to make oil and water mix, to make irreconcilable positions cohere; and much of the best writing in *Making Integral*, including Keatinge's own brilliant contributions, are doomed attempts to believe Richard Murphy – or to make us believe him. The stunning photograph that forms the cover of this book is an astonishing key to the subject-matter within: an oratory window made from different kinds of cut stone that are only reconciled in their architectural purpose. Only the architecture makes them fit together. Murphy's entire life was illuminated by that insight: he was forever making things in order to make this Anglo-Irish world bearable, whether it was restoring and sailing old Galway hookers or rebuilding fallen island homes. It is nearly always through restoration projects that aristocrats integrate with the society around them; people grow fond of each other through common tasks. And indeed, Murphy did grow fond of people, especially Clifden people; as they in turn grew fond of him. His affection for people, from the Concannons to Tony White, is a persistent trope of his life and his poems. A lot of love surrounded him, and he harvested that love greedily. This magnificent book from Cork University Press is probably one of the last great flowerings of that love.

This study of Richard Murphy offers unique opportunities for the luminous display of a new kind of Anglo-Irish criticism; the most effective essays here are vectored and disturbing in their surgery. Philip Keel Geheber gets to the core of such study in his lucid analysis of Murphy's use of place and space, while Michael A Moir, Jr internationalises or colonises the habit of integration of experience in Murphy's memory and poetic method. Moir's nailing of the poet's fluid geography is particularly brilliant. Both of these essays are a new kind of criticism, disciplined by a new critical training. The Murphy family background of colonising both culture and landscape, that instability of the African space – yet another disabled home-coming – is wonderfully captured by Moir. Such scholars offer the bog-standard Irish reader a new way of approaching what might seem familiar material, but clearly is not. Maurice Harmon, wise and catholic as always, casts a warmer eye across the material, uncovering layers and layers of distress and discontinuity in the Murphy oeuvre. Harmon's overview dovetails well into Lucy Collins' searching analysis of the poet's island life – island as destination, definition, and metaphor.

In terms of the new areas of criticism, postcolonial, gay studies, gender studies, James B Kelley's essay here is an unexpected, sensational addition to the sum of our intelligence in Irish poetry. His 'Exposure and Obscurity: The cruising sonnets in Richard Murphy's The Price of Stone' is quite simply a new kind of critical masterpiece, a critique both riveting and exciting. I remember meeting Dennis O'Driscoll in Dublin in the 1980s as he was receiving chunks of these sonnets from the older, anxious poet. Dennis was enthralled by the work, not just by the sheer masonic genius of the structure, its mental discipline, but by the emotional and personal nakedness of what Murphy was writing. "There's a lot more than building-work being described here," warned Dennis, as I sat back in

Bewley's Café, not necessarily buying his learned pitch. In his *In Search of Poetry*, a book that is a cocktail mix of journal entries, aphorisms, quotations, and poems, Murphy brought the readers of his earlier work closer to the sensuous place of making. This book is the key to *The Price of Stone* and James B Kelley uses that key as well as other readings to create an astonishing essay here, in *Making Integral*. Keatinge's book would be worth its price for Kelley's work alone, though as Murphy was well aware, we must pay a price for everything to which we form an attachment. Was there ever a male Irish poet as pleased with his penis as Richard Murphy? The most important erections in *The Price of Stone* are not Anglo-Irish mansions, but follies of a very human kind. And the ejaculations are not at all of the devout Catholic genre. Kelley hovers above this world of desire, understanding and delineating its structural transformation into monumental sonnets, so that the collection becomes a uniquely new thing in Irish writing, an openly gay work of art. Tara Stubbs, also, in her fine essay 'What Price Stone? The shaping of inheritance into form in Richard Murphy's *The Price of Stone* sonnet sequence', tackles the Elizabeth Bowen-like anxiety for stone implicit in Anglo-Irish memory. Kelley and Stubbs have done sterling work.

But writing of high quality is everywhere in *Making Integral*, not least in the superb, shrewd and knowing steer into Murphy for both the beginner and advanced reader of this poet of islands, rectories, choirs, and stones. As editor, or should we say architect, of this marvellous collection of essays, Benjamin Keatinge has set a new gold standard in the analysis of Irish poetry; and in the capture of its many meanings.

Simon Ó Faoláin

NA BLASCAODAÍ AG CAOINEADH JACKEEN
  – do Ghréagóir Ó Dúill

Seol isteach chugham mar atáim anois
– Mar ataoi anois – thar thaoidí mara,
Thar thaoidí dí, goirteamas sáile,
Beathuisce, pórtair, le gleann na ndeor seo
Curtha díot, tabhair aghaidh mhacánta
Ort féinig inár *rehab* diamhair.

Agus, led' thaibhse thanaí cúbtha
Siar i gcoinne an fhalla sa chúinne
I múchán tí oileánaigh mhairbh
Atá gan doras, díon ná fothain,
Atá gan tine, teas ná cosaint,
Cuir díot anois na harasaí,
An t-allas fuar truaillithe,
Fé anailís géar-léirmheastór':
Gálaí garg-bhriathrach' Eanáir.

Beidh duardáil guardaill chughat ag teacht
– Fuaimthonnta tríd an gcarraig ghlas –
Ó chroí an fhalla isteach id' chluas:
Síothlófar as do chroí an racht.

Simon Ó Faoláin

EL MEMORIOSO

Is mise an file Ceann Fhaolaidh · cúis mhaíte na Niallach, mo mhuintir,
béim namhad ag Cath Mhaigh Rátha · do ghearr díom m'inchinn dearúid,
do leigheas an lia mo chréacht · is ón uair a dhéanas téarnamh
thugas liom gach a chualas, · Gach réimse léinn is éigse
ó Alfa siar go hÓiméige · go cruinn gan ghó, gan tuaiplis,
gur ghnóthaíos an teideal *sapiens* · is scríobhas na leabhair mhóra.

Ach ní scéitheas riamh le héinne · gur chuimhneach liom chomh maith
ach ar chualas roimh an gcath, · gach ar chosc m'inchinn dearúid:
éamh i súile seanóglaigh · – an chéad duine a mharaíos –
agus scáth mo chlaímh ardaithe · ag titim ar a aghaidh,
nó níos sia siar arís · truamhéil impí deirféar
agus bagairt chiúin fir ghaoil · i ndorchadas an tseomra.

Is mise an file Ceann Fhaolaidh · arb ionann anois dó gach oíche
ag cuardach mhil na giniúna · i ndríodar cuach meá.

Simon Ó Faoláin

DOM' MHAC AR BHÁS A CHAIT

Is fíor a deir go mbímid uilig *schooled at forepangs*,
Agus duitse, a mhaoineach, seo chughat anois do chéad fhreang.
D'éag do chaitín dil aréir um meán oíche,
Strainc chráite ar a béal, sínte 'na mún, géaga ag preabadh,
ag tabhairt na gcor, ceal aeir, mar lon dubh báite.
'Sea sháraigh an spealadóir tearmann do theaghlaigh is rug
leis comrádaí suairc 'dhein crónán toirní duit is tú sa chliabhán.
Seo céad fheall an tsaoil ort, ach beidh – is iad ag fás – a thuilleadh,
Gan dul as duit feasta ach iad a sheasamh, buille ar bhuille.

Ach is leor fíric an bháis gan fianaise na fulaingthe mar uafás,
Seo mé anois, ag comhlíonadh mo róil mar thuismitheoir:
Bia, fothain, grá gan srian, agus an bhréag is gá.
Ar maidin bhí sí soiprithe, mar ba ghnách, ina leaba chluthair,
Is bhí sé agat mar shólás gur imigh sí go síochánta ina codladh.

FEATURED POET: PAUL MCCARRICK

Paul McCarrick was born in Athlone, Co Westmeath. He received his MA in Writing from NUI Galway, in a literary environment he once called, in an interview, 'as near a perfect setting as you will get'.

He has described himself as beginning writing at 16 or 17, starting an independent theatre company and turning at that time to the writing of both drama and fiction. The energies of both genres are visible in his poems, with their verve for identifying place and the commonplace.

His poems often work with a vernacular of everyday life that can be both engaging and deceptive: the voice can darken into tones of elegy and regret. In this way his poems are able to render the complication of ordinary lives as they migrate into memory, as in the particularly fine poem here, 'Waiting for the Bomb': an artful drama of memories that survive and occasions that don't.

The child seeking out the past of an older relative – 'up on the high stool / beside you, needling, asking, discovering / new lives already lived before mine' – opens a window on legend as well as the past, on worlds lost to reality and saved by language.

The witty and poignant lines about the legend of a pub being raffled and the bewildered acceptance in the child's mind show the strength of the poem as a transport for generations: 'you / raffled off Des Earls' pub so someone would own it / my puzzlement dismissed with your logic / of it being so obvious, nothing else could have been done.'

Poems of a consciousness created as the poem progresses are notoriously hard to write. All too easily the poem can lose its footing, can lapse into literary retrospect or the sort of intellectualisation such a speaker would never attempt. This poem is consistent, from beginning to end: a wonderful journey through the legends and influences of childhood, but always with a path in mind to something deeper and more challenging.

Those challenges are also met in the second poem 'Walking in Donadea'. A different time-frame, and a different project: but the lyric originality is intact, and the conversational presence of the poem, as in 'Waiting for the Bomb', is impressive and persuasive.

– **Eavan Boland**

Paul McCarrick

WAITING FOR THE BOMB

There is nothing else in the world,
no Leinster Final replays, no family dinners,
nothing as good as being up on the high stool
beside you, needling, asking, discovering
new lives already lived before mine,
In the black and white days as you say,
as I hear all about O'Connell Street
and the girls selling stones on the path,
all dotted in clumped paint, or how you
raffled off Des Earls' pub so someone would own it,
my puzzlement dismissed with your logic
of it being so obvious, nothing else could have been done.
Back when the others were being reared,
you worried about the bombs going off
and what to say to the others because lying to the children
is bad enough but at Christmas of all times
there's no use in that. It came to a head when
Nana God rest her soul made sure Santa
started to visit us in or around the same Christmas Eve
you saved the postman, him, at lunchtime
ruined from doing his job all morning,
and you making sure he had a sit down for himself
as you went down the hill of Parnell Square bringing
everyone the last of the cards and the dollars from Boston.
I'm taken aback, when things were simply done,
gotten over, persevered through. And me only arriving
after the Berlin Wall's fall, the death of history and all that.
The start of something new, like Dylan going electric,
or realising Joni was singing his songs better than him.
I began to share their stars and sun and moon,
turning at the same time, coming around to
picking up bank statements, rejection letters,
and remembering the time we got two packets of iodine tablets
because Nana had died and we all together were safe after that.

WALKING IN DONADEA

There isn't a
signpost for love
nor money
in this place
everything else but the signs

there are memorials
for all kinds of things &
coffee stands & benches
in the middle of a path going nowhere
where people sat & took it in
before they died

so when after a half hour
of circling around conversations
you thought
we were actually lost
there was a pulse to say everything
for fear we wouldn't get the chance again
of the exit that we did chance upon again

there was a long moment
lasting right to now
of me wanting
to stay lost
because then as is now
I cannot
write how
happy or say
how happy I am
because I
cannot
write or say
because I am
happy

& oh God
I'm so happy
& why for
the love of the Lord God
can I not show
you how happy I am
on the page

I don't know
I guess I'll have to keep talking
and keep writing and maybe one day
I'll manage make it feel
close to right

Notes on Contributors

Peter Adair lives in Bangor, Northern Ireland. His poems have appeared in *The Honest Ulsterman*, *PN Review*, *The Galway Review*, *The Bangor Literary Journal*, *Lagan Online*, and elsewhere. In 2016 he won The Funeral Services Northern Ireland Poetry Competition. Two of his poems were shortlisted for The Seamus Heaney Award for New Writing 2018.

B. Anne Adriaens lives in Somerset. Her poetry tends to reflect her interest in alienation and her concerns about the environment. Her publication credits include *Helios Quarterly Magazine*, *Harpur Palate*, the *Glasgow Review of Books*, *Whirlagust: The Yaffle Prize Anthology 2019*, *Thimble Literary Magazine*, and *The Blue Nib*.

Bebe Ashley is most recently published by *Banshee*, *Modern Poetry in Translation*, and the *Poetry Jukebox*. She is a student at the Seamus Heaney Centre for Poetry at Queen's University, Belfast, and began a Ph.D. in British Sign Language Poetry this autumn. She was selected as a 2019/2020 Emerging Writer by The London Library.

Ivy Bannister's books are: *Blunt Trauma* (Goose Lane Editions), a memoir; *Vinegar and Spit* (Astrolabe Press), a collection of poetry; and *Magician* (Poolbeg Press), a collection of short stories. Her plays have been broadcast on RTÉ, and she has written more than fifty pieces for *Sunday Miscellany* and *The Living Word*. Her awards include the Mobil Ireland Playwriting Award, the Francis MacManus Short Story Prize, and the Hennessy Literary Award.

Amanda Bell's publications include *First the Feathers* (Doire Press, 2017), which was shortlisted for the Shine/Strong Award; *Undercurrents* (Alba Publishing, 2016), which won a Haiku Society of America Kanterman Merit Book Award and was shortlisted for a Touchstone Distinguished Books Award; *The Lost Library Book* (Onslaught Press, 2017); and *the loneliness of the sasquatch* from the Irish by Gabriel Rosenstock (Alba Publishing, 2018). She is an assistant editor of *The Haibun Journal*.

Eimear Bourke is a poet and medical student from Co Meath. She practised as a solicitor before returning to education. Her poems are shaped by themes such as memory, interpersonal relationships, and nature. Her work can be read in *Boyne Berries*, *Door is a Jar*, *FourXFour*, and *Automatic Pilot*.

Alison Brackenbury's work has won an Eric Gregory Award, a Cholmondeley Award, and has frequently been broadcast on BBC Radio 3 and 4. Her *Gallop: Selected Poems* was published in 2019 by Carcanet Press.

Beverley Bie Brahic's collection *White Sheets* (CB Editions / Fitzhenry & Whiteside) was a finalist for the 2012 Forward Prize. Her translations include *Apollinaire: the Little Auto* (CB Editions), which won the 2013 Scott Moncrieff Prize, and *Baudelaire: Invitation to the Voyage* (forthcoming from Seagull Books). A Canadian, she lives in Paris. Her latest collection is *The Hotel Eden* (Carcanet Press, 2018).

Deirdre Cartmill is an award-winning poet and writer based in Belfast. She has published two poetry collections, *The Return of the Buffalo* (Lagan Press, 2013), and *Midnight Solo* (Lagan Press, 2004). 'Torn', in this issue, is from her forthcoming third collection. She has recently been the Irish Writers' Centre Community Writer in Residence with Women's Aid, and Artist in Residence at the Belfast International Arts Festival.

Jocelyn Casey-Whiteman is author of the chapbook *Lure*, which received a New York Chapbook Fellowship from the Poetry Society of America. Her poems have appeared in *Boston Review*, *Sixth Finch*, *West Branch*, and elsewhere. She teaches creative writing and yoga in New York City.

John Wedgwood Clarke has published two poetry collections: *Ghost Pot* (2013) and *Landfill* (2017), both with Valley Press. His third collection, *Boy Thing*, is due out in 2020. He regularly collaborates with scientists and other artists on cross-disciplinary projects, and lectures in creative writing at the University of Exeter.

Jack Coughlan was born in Co Carlow. He worked in construction in London, then lived in Italy for two years before moving to Germany to work as a labourer. He studied psychology and subsequently worked for a charity organisation. He has published numerous articles in psychology journals, and his poetry is included in the anthology *Reaching for Mercy*.

Kelly Creighton is a poet, novelist, and short story writer living in Co Down. Her books include *Three Primes* (Lapwing Press, 2013), *The Bones of It* (Liberties Press, 2015), and *Bank Holiday Hurricane* (Doire Press, 2017). *The Sleeping Season* will be published in 2020.

Supriya Kaur Dhaliwal is a poet from the Himalayan town of Palampur, India, who studied at St. Bede's College, Shimla and Trinity College Dublin. Her poems have recently appeared or are forthcoming in *Madras Courier*, *The Bombay Literary Magazine*, *The Lonely Crowd*, *Ambit*, *Poetry Jukebox*, *Banshee*, *The Lifeboat*, and elsewhere. Supriya was one of twelve poets selected for Poetry Ireland's Introductions Series in 2018. She is currently studying for an M.A. in Poetry at the Seamus Heaney Centre for Poetry, Queen's University, Belfast.

Doreen Duffy studied creative writing at Oxford University (online), UCD, and the National University of Ireland, Maynooth. She won The Jonathan Swift Award and was presented with the Deirdre Purcell Cup at the Maria Edgeworth Literary Festival. Shortlisted in 2017 for the Francis MacManus Short Story Prize, her story 'Tattoo' was broadcast on RTÉ Radio One. She is studying for an MA in Creative Writing at DCU.

Tim Dwyer's chapbook is *Smithy Of Our Longings: Poems From The Irish Diaspora* (Lapwing Publications, 2015). His poems have appeared frequently in Irish journals. He recently retired as a psychologist from a women's maximum-security prison in New York State, and now lives in Bangor, Co Down.

Frank Farrelly is from Waterford. His poems have been widely published. He won the inaugural Rush Poetry Prize, and was runner up in the Doolin Prize, the North West Words Poetry Competition, and the Poets Meet Politics Competition. He published a chapbook, *Close To Home*, in 2017. He was selected for the Poetry Ireland Introductions Series in 2019.

Ger Feeney, originally from Waterford, has resided in New Ross, Co Wexford for almost 30 years. A retired Garda, he has had poems published in a number of magazines, including, *The Stinging Fly*, *The Galway Review*, *Outburst*, *Tandem*, *Poetry Nottingham*, *Quantum Leap*, *Revival Literary Journal*, and *Inclement Poetry Magazine*.

Nathan Fidler is a copywriter living and working in Nottingham, writing film and music reviews in his spare time. Looking to find a publisher for a first collection, his poems have previously appeared in *Orbis*, *Interpreter's House*, *The North Magazine*, and other outlets.

Maureen Gallagher's first collection of poetry, *Calling the Tune*, was published by WordsontheStreet Press in 2008. Her poetry has appeared widely in magazines and journals, including *Poetry Ireland Review*, *THE SHOp*, *Cork Literary Review*, and *The Stinging Fly*. She won the Wicklow Writers' Poetry Award in 2008, the Goldsmith Poetry Award in 2011, and the Phizzfest Poetry Award in 2012. She has also been shortlisted for a number of other awards, including the Swift, the iYeats, the Gregory O'Donoghue, and the Hennessy Literary Awards.

Catherine Gander lectures in American literature at Maynooth University. Her publications include *Muriel Rukeyser and Documentary: The Poetics of Connection* (2013), *Mixed Messages: American Correspondences in Visual and Verbal Practices* (with Sarah Garland, 2016), and several essays and reviews on poetry, art, and fiction. She is Chair of the all-island Irish Association for American Studies.

Nicola Geddes, originally from Scotland, is a cellist and music teacher in Co Galway. Her poems have been published widely, and she has won awards and commendations from the Patrick Kavanagh Centre, the Over the Edge New Writer of the Year, and *The Irish Times*.

Richard Hayes is an academic based at Waterford Institute of Technology where he is currently the director of institutional strategy. A graduate of Maynooth College and UCD, he has published a number of articles and essays on Irish and American literature. He is a regular contributor to *Trumpet* and *Poetry Ireland Review*.

Nicola Healey's poems have been published in *Poetry Review, The London Magazine, The Spectator, The Dark Horse*, and are forthcoming in *PN Review*. She won the Seren Christmas Poetry Competition 2018, and is the author of *Dorothy Wordsworth and Hartley Coleridge: The Poetics of Relationship* (Palgrave Macmillan, 2012).

Eoin Hegarty won the Cúirt New Writing Prize and was shortlisted for the Poetry Collection Award in the Listowel Writers' Week Competition, in 2018. In 2019 he was part of a mentorship programme with American poet Sandra Beasley, and took part in the Poetry Introductions Series during the Munster Literature Festival's Cork Spring Poetry Festival. He lives and teaches in Cork.

Marie Herbert is a previously unpublished poet, teacher, and mother, in the UK. Through lyrical narrative poetry she explores the lasting personal impact of historical social policy, stretched over time and space, on the relationship between mothers and daughters, and the continued emotional pull of an unknown Ireland.

Seán Hewitt's debut collection, *Tongues of Fire*, is forthcoming from Jonathan Cape in 2020. His debut pamphlet of poems, *Lantern*, won an Eric Gregory Award in 2019, and was the Poetry Book Society Pamphlet Choice for Summer 2019. He won the Resurgence Prize in 2017, and a Northern Writers' Award in 2016. He lives in Dublin.

Dane Holt is currently completing a Ph.D. at Queen's University, Belfast. In 2019 he was the winner of the inaugural Brotherton Prize. In 2018, he was selected as part of the Poetry Ireland Introduction Series. His poems have appeared in *The Tangerine* and *The Lifeboat*.

Eleanor Hooker has published two poetry collections with Dedalus Press: *A Tug of Blue* (2016), and *The Shadow Owner's Companion* (2012). She holds an M.Phil. (Distinction) in Creative Writing from Trinity College Dublin, and is a Fellow of the Linnean Society of London. She is a helm for Lough Derg RNLI Lifeboat, and she curates the Rowan Tree Readings.

Anne Irwin lives in Galway. She studied English Literature and Philosophy at University College Galway. She is a homeopath and tutor at the Belfast School of Homeopathy. Her poetry has been widely published.

Fred Johnston was born in Belfast, and lives in Galway. In 1972, he received a Hennessy Literary Award for prose. He founded Galway's Cúirt festival in 1986 as a poetry event. Poet, novelist, and short story writer, his most recent collection of poems is *Rogue States* (Salmon Poetry, 2018). He also reviews new poetry.

Seán Kelly's work has appeared in *The Moth, The High Window, Skylight 47, Crannóg,* and *Poetry Ireland Review*. He has previously been short-listed for the Cork Literary Review Poetry Manuscript competition, long-listed in the 2017 Fool for Poetry competition, and was awarded second prize in the 2018 Red Line Poetry Competition. He is CEO of the Everyman, Cork.

Brian Kirk is a poet and short story writer from Dublin. His first poetry collection, *After The Fall,* was published by Salmon Poetry in 2017. His poem 'Birthday' won the Listowel Writers' Week Irish Poem of the Year at the An Post Irish Book Awards 2018.

Zosia Kuczyńska is the author of the poetry pamphlet, *Pisanki* (The Emma Press, 2017). Her work has appeared in *The Tangerine* and *The White Review*. In 2019, she was shortlisted for the Máirtín Crawford Award for Poetry, and was highly commended in the Patrick Kavanagh Poetry Award. She is an IRC postdoctoral research fellow at UCD.

Aoife Lyall is an Irish poet living and working in the Scottish Highlands. Shortlisted for the Wells Festival of Literature Open Poetry Competition 2019, as well as the Hennessy Literary Awards 2016 and 2018, her writing has previously appeared in *Poetry Ireland Review, The Irish Times, Gutter, Acumen, Magma, The Butcher's Dog, The Stinging Fly, Banshee,* and elsewhere. Her debut collection will be published by Bloodaxe Books in 2021.

Angela McCabe is the 2016 winner of the Listowel Writers' Week Poetry Collection Competition. Several of her poems have won prizes and appeared in anthologies and literary magazines. Her first three collections were published by Alba Publishing. Her fourth poetry book is published by Salmon Poetry, and she is working on her fifth.

Paul McCarrick – see page 118.

Thomas McCarthy was born in Co Waterford and educated at University College Cork. He worked for many years at Cork City Libraries before he began to write full-time in 2014. He has won many awards for his poetry, including the Patrick Kavanagh Poetry Award and the Alice Hunt Bartlett Prize. His tenth collection, *Prophecy*, is published by Carcanet Press (2019). He is a former editor of *Poetry Ireland Review*.

Martin Malone lives in north-east Scotland. He has published three poetry collections: *The Waiting Hillside* (Templar Poetry, 2011), *Cur* (2015) and *The Unreturning* (2019), both from Shoestring Press. *Larksong Static: Selected Poems 2005–2020* will be published next year. He is a Teaching Fellow in Creative Writing at Aberdeen University.

Geraldine Mitchell is a Patrick Kavanagh Poetry Award winner. She has published three collections of poems with Arlen House, *World Without Maps* (2011), *Of Birds and Bones* (2014), and *Mountains for Breakfast* (2017). She has lived on the Co Mayo coast for the past twenty years.

Mary Montague's poetry collections are *Black Wolf on a White Plain* (Summer Palace Press, 2001), and *Tribe* (Dedalus Press, 2008). She contributes to *The Guardian*'s 'Country Diary'.

Luke Morgan's debut collection, *Honest Walls*, was published by Arlen House Press in 2016. He is currently working on a second collection. He lives and works as a writer and filmmaker in Galway.

Niamh Nic Ghabhann is Assistant Dean, Research for the Faculty of Arts, Humanities, and Social Sciences at the University of Limerick, and Course Director of the MA Festive Arts at the Irish World Academy of Music and Dance, University of Limerick. Her current research focuses on the built devotional infrastructure of the Roman Catholic church in Ireland between 1830 and 1930. She is currently Vice-Chair of the Irish Humanities Alliance.

Mary O'Donnell writes both poetry and prose. Her poetry collections include *Unlegendary Heroes* (1998), *September Elegies* (2003), and *Those April Fevers* (2015). An eighth collection of poetry – *Massacre of the Birds* – will be published next year by Salmon Poetry. She has recently been awarded a Ph.D. from UCC.

Tá trí leabhar filíochta Gaeilge foilsithe ag **Simon Ó Faoláin**. I measc na ngradam atá buaite aige tá Duais Glen Dimplex, Duais Strong, Duais Bhaitéar Uí Mhaicín, Duais Cholm Cille agus Duais Foras na Gaeilge. An leabhar is déanaí uaidh ná *An Corrmhíol*, aistriúchán Gaeilge ar an dán fada Gàidhlig *A' Mheanbhchuileag* le Fearghas MacFionnlaigh.

Francis O'Hare was born in Newry, Co Down. His first two collections, *Falling into an O* (2007) and *Somewhere Else* (2011), were both published by Lagan Press. In 2011, he also published a collection in the US, with Evening Street Press (Ohio), entitled *Home and Other Elsewheres*. His publication credits include *Poetry Ireland Review, Evening Street Review, The Galway Review, The Glasgow Review*, and *The Yellow Nib*.

Ciarán O'Rourke completed his Ph.D. on the cultural politics of William Carlos Williams in 2019. He curates the online archive, Island's Edge Poetry, and his first collection, *The Buried Breath,* is published by Irish Pages Press.

Helen Pizzey lives on the Dorset coast. Her work has appeared in UK and international literary journals, and been runner-up in the Bridport Prize. Aosdána composer Ian Wilson has set her poetry to music for choral and orchestral works, including for the opening of the Derry Peace Bridge, a commemoration of RMS *Titanic*, and a song-cycle funded by the Meath Foundation in Dublin. Her short collection, *Invisibility for Beginners*, was published in 2018 by Cinnamon Press.

Aoife Reilly lives in Kinvara, Co Galway. Her poetry is published in journals and magazines in Ireland and overseas. She read at the Cúirt International Literature Festival in 2016. Her pamphlet, *Lilac and Gooseberries*, was published by Lapwing Press in 2017. She took part in an artist in residency programme in Sicily in 2018, focusing on writing and music. Her first collection is forthcoming from Doire Press, in 2020.

Jean Riley moved to Pembrokeshire in 2018, the Year of the Sea, from Gloucestershire, where she facilitated poetry workshops and writing and reading groups. In Narberth, she collaborates on film-poems and a new podcast, 'Poetry Pause'. Her work appears in *Envoi*, Aldeburgh Poetry Trust's 'Stuff', *Obsessed with Pipework, The Rialto, Ink Sweat and Tears, Under the Radar, Mslexia*, and *Poetry Salzburg Review*.

Patrick Slevin lives in Stockport. His poems have appeared in *The Cormorant, The Interpreter's House, The Manchester Review, The Bangor Literary Review*, and elsewhere.

Morag Smith is a writer, poet, and European Scot. She lives in Paisley with her family. Her short fiction and poetry have been published in numerous magazines and anthologies, including *New Writing Scotland, Nitrogen House, Crannóg*, and *Gutter*. She is one of four Glasgow Clydebuilt poetry apprentices for 2019-20.

Eilis Stanley is a poet and writer from Ashford, Co Wicklow. She has lived in New York, San Francisco, and London. Since returning to Ireland in 2000, she has been short-listed for or awarded a number of poetry prizes, including Listowel Writers' Week, Strokestown, The Fish, and Bridport.

Jamie Stedmond is an emerging Irish poet and short story writer. He graduated from UCD in 2018 with an MA in Creative Writing. You can find his work in various spaces and journals, including: *Banshee*, *The Tangerine*, *Crannóg*, *Litro Online*, *Abridged*, and *The Honest Ulsterman*.

Colette Tennant has two poetry collections: *Commotion of Wings* (2010) and *Eden and After* (2015), as well as the commentary *Religion in the Handmaid's Tale: a Brief Guide* (2019). Her poem 'Rehearsals' was awarded third place by Billy Collins in the 2019 Fish Publishing International Writing Contest. Her poems have appeared in *Rattle*, *Prairie Schooner*, *Southern Poetry Review*, and elsewhere.

Jessica Traynor's collections are *Liffey Swim* (2014) and *The Quick* (2018), both from Dedalus Press. Forthcoming projects include *Paper Boat*, an opera commissioned by Music for Galway and Galway 2020. She is Carlow Writer in Residence in 2020, and recipient of the 2020 Banagher Public Art Commission. She is a Creative Fellow of UCD.

Grace Wells won the Rupert and Eithne Strong Award with her debut poetry collection, *When God Has Been Called Away to Greater Things* (Dedalus Press, 2010), which was also shortlisted for the London Festival Fringe New Poetry Award. Her second collection *Fur* (Dedalus Press, 2015) was lauded by *Poetry Ireland Review* as 'a book that enlarges the possibilities of poetry'. Her poem 'Otter' received a 2017 Forward Prize.

Máiríde Woods writes poetry and short stories. Her work has appeared in anthologies and reviews, and has been broadcast on RTÉ radio. She has won several prizes, including two Hennessy Awards, and the Francis MacManus and PJ O'Connor awards from RTÉ. Three poetry collections, *The Lost Roundness of the World*, *Unobserved Moments of Change*, and *A Constant Elsewhere of the Mind* have been published by Astrolabe Press.

Enda Wyley's sixth collection, *The Painter on his Bike*, was published by Dedalus Press in November, 2019. She is a member of Aosdána.

Sandra Yannone published her debut collection, *Boats for Women*, with Salmon Poetry in 2019. Salmon Poetry will also publish *The Glass Studio* in 2022. Her poems and reviews have appeared in *Ploughshares*, *Live Encounters*, *The Stony Thursday Book*, *Prairie Schooner*, and *Women's Review of Books*. She lives in Olympia, Washington.